LEADING

NOT NORMAL

VOLUNTEERS

A NOT NORMAL GUIDE FOR LEADING
YOUR INCREDIBLE, QUIRKY TEAM

SUE MILLER & ADAM DUCKWORTH

orange

Leading Not Normal Volunteers:
A Not Normal Guide for Leading Your Incredible, Quirky Team

www.NotNormalBook.com

Published by Orange, a division of The reThink Group, Inc.
5870 Charlotte Lane, Suite 300
Cumming, GA 30040 U.S.A.

The Orange logo is a registered trademark of The reThink Group, Inc.

All Scripture quotations, unless otherwise noted, are taken from the Holy Bible, New International Version®. NIV®. Copyright © 1973, 1978, 1984 by International Bible Society. Used by permission of Zondervan.

Other Orange products are available online and direct from the publisher. Visit our website at www.ThinkOrange.com for more resources like these.

ISBN: 978-1-941259-51-1

©2016 Sue Miller and Adam Duckworth

Lead Editor: Mike Jeffries
Art Direction: Ryan Boon
Project Coordinator: Nate Brandt
Design: Sharon van Rossum

Printed in the United States of America

First Edition 2016

4 5 6 7 8 9 10 11 12 13

05/26/2016

Copies of this book are available for distribution in churches, schools, and other venues at a significant quantity discount. For more details, go to www.OrangeStore.org.

CONTENTS

FOREWORD

So you lead volunteers.

You're our favorite kind of leader. You get to engage on a daily, weekly, and monthly basis with those who believe in what it means to be "Not Normal." You understand the most important thing you will ever do related to leadership is to invest in the lives of those that you lead.

You understand that even if you are the leader of a kids ministry that you don't really lead kids – you lead volunteers.

You understand that even if you are the leader of a student ministry that you don't really lead students – you lead volunteers.

You understand that if you are in charge of the parking lot–yeah, you care how people get their car parked–but you are really responsible for the volunteers you lead.

When we wrote *Not Normal: Seven Quirks of Incredible Volunteers*, we wrote an entire book to your volunteers telling them how to step up their game so they could get the most out of their serving. We encouraged them to take their volunteering to the next level.

Now it's your turn. Week in and week out, you are the person who can step up your game to help them do what they do to the best of their ability. We know what a daunting task that is. That's why we want to help you do it.

This past year, we've met many of you and listened to your stories and the challenges you're facing with volunteers. Some common questions keep emerging as you work hard to develop "Not Normal" volunteers.

Questions like:

How do you recruit more volunteers?

How do you turn renters into owners?

What do you do with volunteers who are difficult to deal with?

Why would volunteers stay engaged with the program that I lead for multiple years?

What is a coaching structure and why do I need it?

I work by myself — how in the world am I supposed to lead this entire department of volunteers?

The two of us have more than fifty years of combined experience in leading volunteers. But we didn't want to be content with just what we know. We asked other leaders to give us their best thinking as well. There's simply too much at stake to just take our word for it. Because, let's be honest, without you and what you do there would be no . . .

compelling visions for volunteers to get behind.

schedules so they know where to be when and what to do.

encouragement so they keep on going.

stories told that keep their hearts understanding why they do what they do.

Your volunteers are important. They are essential. They have skills, wisdom, experience, and the desire to do something significant with them. You couldn't do ministry without these volunteers.

But you are important, too. You are essential to them. They couldn't do what they do without you. They need a leader who will help them get their skills in the game to do something much bigger than they are.

That's why we wrote this leaders edition, so that you would be encouraged, inspired, and equipped in your role. With the volunteer version in their hands (available in quantity discounts so they're available for your entire team) and this leaders edition in your hands, you'll have a training tool that will make an immediate difference in your ministry. As you go through this book, you'll see that it's perfectly matched chapter-by-chapter to amplify what your volunteers are reading.

We want to set you up to win. Hopefully, this will help you simplify and streamline what you need to do so the "Not Normal" volunteers you love so much will thrive while serving.

Sue Miller and Adam Duckworth

CHAPTER 1

START SOMEWHERE

THE SCOOP

The volunteer edition of **Not Normal** *features seven different quirks of truly incredible volunteers. This first quirk is a fairly simple one, but one of the most meaningful if we are to begin living not normal lives: Start Somewhere.*

Most of us start out really wanting to do something that matters with our lives.

Then we get busy. Then just when we can manage how busy we are, we get comfortable.

COMFORTABLE LIVING THE STATUS QUO

COMFORTABLE FOCUSED ON OUR OWN NEEDS AND INTERESTS

COMFORTABLE WITH OUR CURRENT ROUTINES

This all feels quite normal.

But along the way, every now and then, we sense that something is missing. Something more important than all of this everyday stuff. Something much bigger. Something that's going to outlast our time on this planet.

Every one of us dreams about giving ourselves to an important cause. We imagine how great it would be to change something in the world that would make life

(WHAT WE TOLD YOUR VOLUNTEERS)

better for someone else. We long to give ourselves to something bigger than our own lives and interests.

Needs are all around us each and every day. Some of them are really big needs, and some are really small needs. Some of these needs happen at our churches, and some of them happen in our communities, and some happen in other countries. Some happen with people we know and some happen with complete strangers.

THERE IS A NOT NORMAL MISSION THAT WILL CAPTURE YOUR HEART AND YOUR IMAGINATION.

THERE IS A NOT NORMAL ORGANIZATION THAT CAN SHOW YOU HOW TO CHANGE SOMEONE ELSE'S WORLD.

THERE IS A NOT NORMAL LIFE FILLED WITH PURPOSE AND FULFILLMENT LIKE YOU'VE NEVER EXPERIENCED BEFORE.

It's simpler than you think.

Which takes us back to Not Normal Quirk Number One:

TAKE ONE SMALL STEP AND JUST START VOLUNTEERING SOMEWHERE.

RUN WITH IT

(HOW YOU HELP YOUR VOLUNTEERS DO IT)

1. MAKE IT EASY

Starting to volunteer in your church or organization should be one of the easiest things that a person can do. There needs to be a system in place to keep things safe for sure (more about that later), but if you put a whole bunch of obstacles in the way of people beginning to volunteer with you, they may walk away before they start.

We have heard of churches that require lengthy membership processes before anyone can plug in to the most simple of volunteer positions. Sometimes, someone just wants to check something out to see if it is for them. We have heard of first-time volunteers having to go through . . .

6-WEEK CLASSES

10-HOUR SATURDAY ORIENTATIONS

COMMITMENT CONTRACTS

CONSULTATIONS WITH THE DEPARTMENT DIRECTOR WITH ACCUSATORY QUESTIONS

FINGERPRINTED BACKGROUND CHECKS WITH SEVEN PERSONAL REFERENCES

All to be a DOOR GREETER!

Instead, make the first step for a volunteer easy.

START WITH A CONVERSATION.

It's personal, relational, non-threatening, and inviting to anyone interested in volunteering with you. It shows them immediately that you already think they are worth investing in.

This is hands down
the most effective strategy
out there today.

What if there is no one to invite to coffee, besides your family, and they're already volunteering every week? What if there's no waiting list of happy people anxious and ready to make a not normal difference in some else?

You can't let that stop you. No names to pursue? Then it's time to go after some!

GET NAMES FROM KEY INFLUENCERS IN YOUR CHURCH.

Ask them to recommend some people who aren't serving already and might be open to a new opportunity.

NETWORK WITH KEY PARENTS.

ASK WHO DOES COMMUNITY THEATER.

FIND OUT WHICH MIDDLE, HIGH SCHOOL, AND COLLEGE STUDENTS HAVE A REPUTATION OF BEING GREAT WITH KIDS.

WHO HAS DONE VBS OR HIGH SCHOOL CAMP IN THE PAST?

WHO WORKS PART-TIME IN THE LOCAL PARK DISTRICT?

LISTEN FOR NAMES OF FAVORITE TEACHERS WHO GO TO YOUR CHURCH.

Oh yeah, and please don't forget to ask for names of senior adults in your church. Many of them are looking for a place to make a difference during retirement. You've just got to find them.

THEN, FROM THAT LIST OF NAMES, INVITE A FEW TO HAVE COFFEE WITH YOU.

Your treat.

Choose a place that feels safe, comfortable, and convenient for your guest. After all, you want the right atmosphere to cue up a relaxed and easy conversation.

Wondering what you're going to talk about? So glad you asked . . . see our second suggestion on the next page.

2. BECOME AN EXPERT AT CASTING VISION

Sometimes you and I are good at meeting new potential volunteers, but then we stumble all over our words when trying to articulate our ministry vision. WE know what we are trying to say, but we might be the only ones!

Sometimes we even resort to talking about the need we have to fill because it's urgent and simpler to articulate. We pitch the hole that desperately needs to be filled. Ever done that? Just filling in the blanks and checking the box? Then, on the drive home, we realize that we just asked an incredibly awesome person to become a hole-filler. Yikes. Nobody wants to be a hole-filler. Ain't nobody got time for that! Volunteers want to make a difference, not fill a hole.

REMEMBER THESE VERY WISE WORDS: "WHERE THERE IS NO VISION, THE PEOPLE PERISH." (PROVERBS 29:18, KJV)

Vision helps people see what your ministry could look like one day. Vision paints a word picture that shows how someone's world will be better because of what you are doing together. It gives people hope that the future can be better than the present—and they can be part of that.

Vision stirs passion in people. It feels significant, even world-changing. It makes volunteers get up out of bed on their day off and show up to serve someone else for free. Week after week. Vision is that important. Without it, ministries stagnate and die. And volunteers' hopes and dreams die with them.

So, as leaders, we have to get better and better at talking about our vision in order to draw others to it and breathe life and vitality into those we serve alongside of.

Let's make vision easy. Easy for you, and the person sitting across the table in conversation with you.

Easy to:

UNDERSTAND (What compelling problem are you trying to solve?)

ACTIVATE (What can one person do to help you solve that problem?)

COMMUNICATE (What is going to be better in the future if you can accomplish this mission?)

When my (Sue) senior pastor, Bill Hybels, was recruiting me to become the children's ministry director for Promiseland at Willow Creek Community Church, the words he chose to recruit me were deal-makers or deal-breakers (though he certainly didn't know that at the time.)

If Bill had asked me to leave my teaching career in the public school system to tweak and maintain their current children's ministry program, I would have said no. Absolutely no. Beyond a shadow of a doubt, no. Nothing about that rings my bell whatsoever. I am not wired to be a maintainer.

But I knew God was behind my job change when Bill asked me to come and build a national-caliber children's ministry for the sake of reaching unchurched kids and discipling them.

Wow. That vision of trying to build the best possible children's ministry in order to reach kids and families who don't go to church struck a deep chord inside me. That challenge excited me, even though I had no idea what that would even look like.

TRYING TO FIGURE IT OUT MADE MY HEART START TO RACE AND TOTALLY ENERGIZED ME.

I imagined kids dragging their parents out of bed on a Sunday morning asking them to get in the car and take them to church. Those kids didn't want to miss a single minute of what was going to be happening there, because they loved it! I pictured a children's ministry where the kids were taught the Bible in creative and engaging ways, sitting on the edge of their seats listening to the story the whole time. I longed for a place where every child was a part of a small circle of friends, an inclusive small group led by a consistent leader who loved them and knew them. Instead of children's ministry being a place that most people would say they survived, I wanted our ministry to be the BEST hour of every kid's week.

This vision kept me up at night. I believed every child needed to grow up with a faith in a really big God. Bill's visionary words not only recruited me, they literally yanked me right out of my teaching career and into the ministry ride of my life.

We want you to
be able to stir up
that kind of motivation
in others too.

Some people you take to coffee would have never considered serving on your team until they heard your vision. God is going to ignite a passion in them that they had never experienced before.

WORDS MATTER.

Practice your "vision words" over and over again until you can say them in a way that will excite someone else. Figure out how to text them, email them, or tweet them, so you are ready when the opportunity presents itself. Believe that the God who has called you to your mission is going to give you who you need to get the job done. He has all the volunteers you and I will ever need . . . on speed dial.

3. MAKE FRIENDS, NOT CLIENTS

From your very first encounter, be volunteer-centered. You have to truly believe that asking someone to volunteer on your team is in their best interest, so treat them that way right from the get-go. In every part of your communication with a potential volunteer, look for ways to value them. Ask them to tell you their story. Inquire about their job or their current school year. Find out what things they enjoy doing. Listen for clues about their strengths so you can see where they might fit best. Explain what benefits are in it for them personally. Try to help them see how much there is to gain from investing in someone else's life.

When people think that you are just having coffee with them to plug them into your ministry, it sounds more like a sales pitch than an engaging conversation. And we all know how sales pitches go.

If your volunteers feel like they are just getting a sales pitch as they begin, they probably won't stay.

WORK ON HOW YOU SAY WHAT YOU SAY.

Engage with them about their personal life before you make an ask. Look them in the eyes.

AND MOST OF ALL, ALWAYS ALLOW THEM TO THINK ABOUT THE DECISION TO SERVE BEFORE YOU ASK FOR THEIR SIGNATURE ON THE DOTTED LINE. THEY WILL FEEL MORE VALUED IF YOU DO.

4. HAVE SERVICE OPTIONS

We know you may have an ideal scenario for a volunteer that you are looking for (every week, totally consistent small group leaders, right?) But often you have to give people a place to just start and let them grow into a bigger commitment.

FIRST, YOU JUST WANT TO GET THEM IN THE FRONT DOOR SO THAT THEY CAN EXPERIENCE WHAT HAPPENS IN YOUR MINISTRY. BE CREATIVE ON THIS ONE.

What if they can't serve every week?

ASSURE THEM THAT THERE IS A PLACE WHERE THEY CAN START AND SERVE EVERY OTHER WEEK.

What if they can't serve the whole hour?

GIVE THEM AN IDEA OF THE ROLES THAT ARE AVAILABLE BEFORE OR AFTER YOUR GATHERING TIME.

Could they be a greeter? Help with registration or administration? Serve on a team during weekdays? Be on your First Impressions team and help people find their way to where they are going?

What if they say they have no time at all?

ASK IF IT WOULD BE OKAY TO PUT THEM ON YOUR "SPECIAL EVENTS LIST" OF VOLUNTEERS.

This special events list only serves three or four times all year. People like this help serve during extremely busy seasons of ministry like before a retreat or a camp. You always need an extra hand for the Christmas Eve services or over summer break. It's a bite-sized schedule commitment, but it's still a place that allows a volunteer to get started. They have their foot in the door, and that's a good thing. They're *starting somewhere*.

You don't know what the future holds for you or that volunteer.

They may fall in love with the role they play and later be open to increasing their availability. But even if they don't, they are still on your team. You still have an opening with them and your entire ministry gains from their influence and experience.

On the other hand, be ready to make your biggest ask to those that seem ready for it. Some people are ready to become consistent every-week small group leaders right out of the gate. They get why it matters and want to jump in to make a significant difference. Buy these people a pastry or something chocolate to go along with their coffee right then and there if you get this kind of response!

Having volunteer job descriptions thought through in advance will help you determine what kind of commitment you're asking for. When you think about service options, remember this: No matter how often volunteers serve, or what role they play, every job description needs to be significant, clear, and focused.

SIGNIFICANT (Every role is critically important in order to achieve the mission.)

CLEAR (Every volunteer needs to know how to win in their role.)

FOCUSED (Volunteers serve doing something they enjoy.)

Leaders often try to create beefy volunteer roles so we will need fewer people to accomplish our mission. We throw everything but the kitchen sink at them. When they show up to serve, volunteers get overwhelmed. Sometimes they quit because they don't feel like they are doing anything well. It's hard for them to feel like they are winning at anything when doing that much multi-tasking.

WHEN JOB DESCRIPTIONS ARE NARROW AND FOCUSED, THEN THE RIGHT PEOPLE END UP SERVING IN THE RIGHT PLACES AND THAT'S ALWAYS A BIGGER WIN FOR YOU AND THEM.

Close your conversation by giving the person several days to think about what you've talked about. Don't pressure them to make an instant decision. Ask if it would be okay if you gave them a call later in the week to check back. Thank them for their time and for sharing their story.

Then, pray like crazy that God will do what only He can do and bring the right volunteers to your ministry.

TRUST HIM WITH THE OUTCOME FOR EACH PERSON YOU TALK WITH.

5. SYSTEMS ARE ESSENTIAL FOR NEWBIES

For those very special people who say yes, you now have a chance to impress them with your quality follow-up and follow-through. You want them to feel like they've joined a winning team in your ministry, so their assimilation needs to be a positive experience. Aim to create raving fans from your newbies.

Too many times, those initial opportunities are lost. We've talked to volunteers who . . .

EXPRESSED INTEREST IN SERVING, BUT NEVER RECEIVED A CALL BACK.

WERE PLACED IN A ROOM WHERE THEY DIDN'T FEEL WELCOME.

HAD NO EARTHLY IDEA WHAT THEY WERE SUPPOSED TO DO ALL HOUR.

What went wrong here?

A LEADER HAD AN EPIC RECRUITMENT STRATEGY TO GET NEEDED PEOPLE, BUT WASN'T PREPARED WITH A FOLLOW-UP PLAN. (ALMOST LIKE WE DIDN'T PLAN FOR SUCCESS, RIGHT?)

A LEADER HAD NO IDEA THAT SHE PLACED NEW VOLUNTEERS IN A ROOM WITH SEASONED VOLUNTEERS IN CONFLICT. OOPS!

A LEADER WAS UNDER PRESSURE TO FILL A SLOT SO THEY STUCK A NEWBIE IN A ROOM WITH NO TRAINING BEFOREHAND.

Funny, isn't it? We work ridiculously hard to track down new people and recruit them, but then we don't work just as hard to KEEP them! We drop the ball at a critical play in our strategy with volunteers.

MAYBE IT'S TIME FOR US TO DO OUR HOMEWORK AND COME UP WITH A WELL-DESIGNED ASSIMILATION PLAN BEFORE WE RECRUIT ANYONE NEW.

Maybe we need to find out from our current volunteers what their experience was like starting out, and get their suggestions on how to improve our system for new volunteers.

Think through these four questions:

1. WHAT DO THEY NEED TO KNOW BEFORE THEY SET FOOT IN THEIR NEW ROLE?

If safety and security policies are part of your process, help the new leader know why what you are asking is important so they know the why behind the what.

2. WHEN IS THE MOST CONVENIENT TIME FOR THEM TO GET BASIC TRAINING SO THEY WILL KNOW WHAT THEY ARE DOING ON THEIR FIRST DAY?

We don't want to take them away too many times before they start to serve. How can we make this easy for them? Podcast? Video? Have them shadow an expert volunteer already serving?

3. WHO WILL INTRODUCE THEM TO THE PEOPLE THEY WILL BE SERVING WITH?

Do you know how the team of volunteers who are already serving in that room or area are doing? Are they happy campers? Any homework need to be done in there by you in advance of the new introduction? Talk about huddle time being a place where volunteers connect and care for each other.

4. ONCE THE NEWBIE IS PLACED IN THEIR NEW DIGS, WHEN WILL YOU CHECK BACK WITH THEM?

We recommend some predictable rhythms of follow up with each new volunteer. Check back in with them at three weeks, six months, and then a year to find out if they are enjoying their role. Ask if there is any obstacle holding them back in their current role. You will be surprised at what you will learn from their answers. Most of the time their obstacles are easy things to remedy, and when you can act on their requests, volunteers feel "heard" and well-served.

SYSTEMS FOR LARGER TEAMS OF VOLUNTEERS

The system of care we just described works well when you have one to ten volunteers. But things start to break down when you try to care for more than ten people. You can't keep up with what is going on in their lives. It's too many people to get feedback from, and too many for you to be able to follow up with their requests. Balls start to drop, things get forgotten, and volunteers begin to fall through the cracks relationally.

With a larger team, a volunteer leadership coaching structure will help avoid all of that.

HERE'S HOW IT WORKS:

1. THE FIRST TEN PEOPLE HAVE YOU AS THEIR COACH.

Your role each week is to circle them up and lead huddle time with them. You encourage, sup-port, and connect them one to another. You keep them in the loop with pertinent information. While they are serving, you troubleshoot for them.

2. WHEN YOU HAVE MORE THAN TEN, ASK SOMEONE IN THAT CIRCLE TO TAKE OVER AS COACH.

Do the hand-off transition well with your first volunteer coach. Then get ready to move out of that circle and start a new one.

3. YOU START TO COACH THE NEXT TEN INCOMING VOLUNTEERS.

When that group grows to ten, do the same thing again. Ask one of them to become the coach for that group, transition, and then move out again to start the next circle of incoming ten.

All of the coaches report to you for their care, value, and development. These men and women are your key influencers, so choose them wisely and invest in them regularly. They will be the ones who will give you great feedback on what changes the volunteers want to see made. These coaches can keep the vision alive each week, living out your team values so people don't lose sight of what you are all trying to do. Their excitement, passion, and enthusiasm keeps momentum going as they pour into the volunteers under their care. Coaches also step in to resolve conflict when needed, or can ask you to step in and mediate a really tough situation.

COACHES ALLOW MINISTRY TO GROW BIG AND STILL OFFER GREAT VOLUNTEER CARE.

Even when your ministry grows over time, this coaching structure allows your care ratios to be small enough to function well. It allows you to build depth in your leadership ranks as well, so other great leaders can help you lead your team wisely and strategically.

When you first connect with someone relationally, you treat them like your friend, not your client. From that moment on, you want to do your best to provide what your volunteers need in order to serve with you over the long haul. Value and care never go out of style. Both remind volunteers that they matter, not because of what they do, but because of who they are.

CHAPTER 2

SMALL IS BIG

THE SCOOP

The smallest things we do can have the biggest results. Not normal results.

It starts by understanding that every. . .

CARD YOU SEND

PHONE CALL YOU MAKE

BIRTHDAY YOU REMEMBER

GAME YOU ATTEND

ENCOURAGING WORD YOU SAY

HAND YOU HOLD

OR TEAR YOU WIPE AWAY

can mean more than you could ever imagine.

These aren't the moments that are going to increase your bank account, get you a luxury automobile, or cause you to become the CEO of a major corporation. We think it is fine for folks who achieve that status, but the moments we are talking about help you achieve a different type of status. The not normal kind.

Our culture talks about that other kind of BIG all the time. The way it is highlighted in our world today, it's easy to believe those achievements will make our lives feel richer and more fulfilled.

(WHAT WE TOLD YOUR VOLUNTEERS)

That's the promise, at least, until you actually get all of those things and put your head on the pillow at night wondering why you still have that empty feeling deep down inside.

The answer you are looking for can be found in the quirky small things you do for someone else as you volunteer. They seem small and simple at the time, but definitely have the biggest return overall.

You know why?

Jesus gave us the answer to this. He taught that when someone needs your help to go one mile, you should go two miles instead. He wanted us to go the extra mile. Unconditionally. We do this not because we have to, but because we want to. Not because of a paycheck, but with no expectations of anything in return.

RUN WITH IT

(HOW YOU HELP YOUR VOLUNTEERS DO IT)

1. MAKE THE DIFFERENCE DOABLE

As leaders, we often contribute unknowingly to volunteers feeling insignificant. We don't mean to, but we do.

You see, we live in the world of BIG.

We are naturally drawn to the 40,000-foot view of our entire ministry. We see the big picture in our mind, and it excites us. So we talk about . . .

BIG GOALS
BIG IDEAS
BIG IMPACT

And those things are all important when leading others.

BUT, we forget that our volunteers mostly serve week to week in the SMALL.

SMALL TASKS

SMALL ROLES

SMALL LIFE-CHANGE

Our job as leaders is to constantly remind them that it takes lots of small steps to make the big things happen. When we connect these dots, we make the difference achievable.

Volunteers often go home feeling like it was no big deal to . . .

SHARE HOW GOD ANSWERED YOUR PRAYER WITH A SMALL CIRCLE OF FOUR-YEAR-OLDS.

SPEND A FRIDAY NIGHT LOCKED IN WITH MIDDLE SCHOOL STUDENTS.

HAVE COFFEE WITH A HIGH SCHOOLER TALKING THROUGH AN UNWISE CHOICE.

At the end of their serving time, they had nothing BIG to show for it.

NO BIG LIFE CHANGE HAPPENED.

NO ONE MADE A SALVATION DECISION.

NO ONE MADE A GREAT CHOICE.

Can you see how easily volunteers can equate what they do with the small?

Imagine if that's how ministry looks to them for a whole year? How significant do you think they would feel by then? Vision leaks out over time, and pretty soon your vision bucket is empty. You can't remember why you ever signed up for this crazy thing in the first place. What were you thinking!

UNTIL A LEADER PUTS IT IN PERSPECTIVE AND CONNECTS THE SMALL TO THE BIG:

Four-year-olds are wide open to believing that God answers their prayers. We want them to grow up hearing how He does that year after year. That's a foundational faith step.

Middle school students need to have fun and build trust with their small group leader. That's how they will feel free enough to process their doubts about their own faith, a critical growth step for them during these years.

As a high school student, it's important to know that God still loves me when I make a mistake, and so does my small group leader. For that high school student to experience unconditional love is a game changer during these years. Don't we want them to grow up feeling like their church is the safest place to process their mistakes and grow from them?

NONE OF THESE STEPS WOULD HAVE HAPPENED WITHOUT A VOLUNTEER.

Big faith is the collection of hundreds of small steps. Volunteers need you to connect the dots for them between these two. That's how you will convince them that they will make a difference.

Make the difference doable.

2. PAY THE POSTAGE

If we really believe in this idea of "Small is ... volunteers how important it is so do small thin... big difference, then we have to support them when the... do it.

This means if you want them to send birthday cards and other random greetings to the kids and teenagers they lead, you should pay the postage.

Not you personally.

But from your budget.

So often, we put too much on our volunteers. An example of this is expecting them to pay the postage on cards that they send. Not only should you pay the postage, but it is also a good idea to buy the cards. (Think of how little that costs, and how much value it communicates.)

Of course, that's just one example.

CONSIDER IT YOUR RESPONSIBILITY AS A LEADER TO HELP MAKE YOUR VOLUNTEERS LOOK GOOD, ESPECIALLY WHEN IT'S AS SIMPLE AS BUYING A ROLL OF POSTAGE STAMPS.

You want them to be successful in their role. Whenever you think of ways to make it easy for a volunteer to encourage a student or a parent, you set them up to win.

Look for key volunteers who do this value really well. These volunteers are gifted at encouraging and helping others feel valued. Get their ideas and make them available to everyone else, so those who struggle with this or don't have the time to think of these ideas will feel the win as well.

. SHOW UP TO A BALL GAME

THE REASON WE BELIEVE IN THE IDEA OF LEADING SMALL IS BECAUSE WE BELIEVE THAT WHAT ONE DOES FOR A FEW HAS MORE OF AN IMPACT THAN WHAT ONE CAN DO FOR MANY.

As we (Adam's church) were implementing the concept of leading small in Fort Lauderdale, I knew that I could never hit every kid's basketball game. That's why we encouraged small group leaders to do that when they were able. But just because I couldn't do it for everyone doesn't mean I didn't do it occasionally.

Your volunteers need to know from time to time that you are in the trenches with them too.

When you do this you are able to put some change in your pocket as is it related to your volunteers. They might even look at you and say, "Isn't this my job? Why are you here?" And if they say that, you know you did an awesome job vision-casting (like we talked about in the first chapter). A great response to that question might be "Yes, this is your job. Thanks for letting me be on your turf. I just want you to know that I support you so I show up to partner alongside you from time to time."

That volunteer will feel supported, loved, and appreciated. And they would feel like you, the leader, are putting your money where your mouth is.

It isn't just limited to ball games.

SHOW UP TO MILESTONE EVENTS.

SHOW UP TO SPECIAL OCCASIONS.

INTERACT WITH KEY FAMILIES TO CHECK THE PULSE OF THE MINISTRY.

Show up

EVERY WEEK.

This is so essential if you are going to lead volunteers to understand that Small is Big. One of the smallest things that volunteers do that has the biggest results is to show up every week. As the leader, you should be present in your department every single week. Furthermore, you should try to be the first person to show up each week so you are the first face they see.

THESE SMALL THINGS THAT YOU CAN DO WILL HELP THEM UNDERSTAND HOW BIG THE SMALL THINGS REALLY ARE.

Want to go big on leading small? We recommend *Lead Small*, a book by our friends Reggie Joiner and Tom Shefchunas that explains this even more. Get your copy at: www.OrangeStore.org

4. LOOK FOR WAYS TO HELP OTHERS

We recently met a warm, athletic-looking Student Ministry Director while teaching at Live to Serve. (Live to Serve is our regional conference for leaders like you and volunteers like the ones you lead. Coming soon to your city! But back to our story . . .) Dan asked if he could share his ministry journey over the past two years. We are so glad we said yes! He told us a story we have honestly never heard before in twenty years of ministry. It illustrates the importance of this principle in a fresh new way.

Two years ago, Dan was hired to lead a student ministry that had been declining for a couple of years. None of the senior leaders knew why.

Dan wondered, too.

WAS THEIR MEETING TIME INCONVENIENT FOR STUDENTS?

WAS THE PROGRAMMING LAME?

WERE THE VOLUNTEERS APATHETIC?

WAS THERE A STRATEGY IN PLACE?

WAS THE ENVIRONMENT AN OBSTACLE?

IT TOOK HIM ONE MONTH TO DIAGNOSE THE PROBLEM, NO ROCKET SCIENCE NEEDED:

Out of the eight volunteers he had, one was a big financial giver to the church.

The ringleader was a woman with a powerhouse personality who was very vocal and opinionated.

One dad was an influential board member.

ALL of them were complainers. Dan nicknamed them the "NO" people.

NO TO DAN BEING THEIR LEADER.

NO TO TRYING A NEW SMALL GROUP STRATEGY.

NO TO CHANGING THEIR MEETING TIME ONE HOUR EARLIER EACH WEEK.

Just no. To everything and anything new. NO!

DAN THOUGHT ABOUT HIS OPTIONS:

ASK THEM TO LEAVE ONE AT A TIME AND START OVER WITH NEW BLOOD.

CONFRONT EACH ONE OVER COFFEE AND CHALLENGE THEM TO CHANGE.

QUIT AND LOOK FOR A JOB CLOSER TO A BEACH.

We were prepared for him to choose any one of the three options from above. But his choice floored us. He decided to see if he could change their attitude and behavior and win them over. His course of action? Love and serve them generously. Model the behavior he wanted to see in them.

We thought for sure he was going to say, "quit and move closer to the beach." What a huge challenge to take on as a young leader. Dan started actively looking for ways to help each one of them wherever they were at. Here are some ways he helped them (and himself):

FIRST STEP IN THE PROCESS, GET TO KNOW THEM AS INDIVIDUALS. SEPARATE THEM FROM THE NEGATIVITY OF THE WHOLE GROUP.

Over coffee, he asked about their jobs, families, and current challenges.

He also wanted to let them get to know him as well. Each one asked him why he came to their church. They wanted to hear his story.

So he shared with them how he and his wife had prayed and agonized over this decision. It had been one of the toughest decisions they had faced in their young marriage so far. Their house sold in record time, which was wonderful, but also very emotional for his wife. Moving meant saying goodbye to her family in that area. Her family was close and provided great support for their two preschoolers. No one wanted to leave the grandparents behind.

But they were both positive that this was where they were supposed to be.

Dan said every time he shared their story, it felt like the volunteers' hearts grew one size bigger. God was clearly working in all of this. So he kept at it.

Here's another step he took:

DAN STARTED TEXTING EACH ONE DURING THE WEEK ASKING THEM HOW THEY WERE.

Sometimes, that led to unexpected opportunities.

When the influential board member's car would not start one icy cold night in January, Dan volunteered to drive the influential board member home.

When powerhouse personality's high schooler was hospitalized with a basketball injury, Dan mobilized some moms and created a meal train for their family.

Another way he helped:

DAN WALKED AROUND ASKING IF HE COULD HELP WITH ANYTHING WHILE VOLUNTEERS WERE SERVING THEIR STUDENTS.

He paid attention to the smallest details. Sometimes, he would just run and get them a water bottle in order to let them know he was there to support them.

Dan's wife, Judy, made her soon-to-become-famous homemade cookies for their team of eight to enjoy during huddle time. Dan gave the huddle one new example each week of why it's important for high school students to have another adult in their lives during these four years.

He made minimal changes that first year to the student ministry, concentrating instead on building a volunteer community that would love and serve each other generously first. After all, how could volunteers hope to pass that kind of student environment on unless they had experienced it themselves first?

NINE MONTHS LATER, THINGS STARTED TO FEEL DIFFERENT.

One night during huddle time, the powerhouse personality asked Dan what he thought needed to change in order to attract new students.

Two of Dan's volunteers invited his wife out to lunch one day. They wanted to befriend her, knowing she missed her family back home.

There was a noticeable lack of complaining from his group of eight. They weren't joyful or triumphant yet, but there were smidges of positivity starting to pop up here and there during huddle time.

Every now and then someone would ask another volunteer if there was something they could do to help.

Dan and Judy could both feel the tide turning. All of the small things that been done to help these volunteers started to add up to a much bigger impact.

High school students who walked into their ministry environment were met by volunteers actively looking for ways to help them. There was a generosity of spirit, love, and kindness towards one another that made their space an irresistible place to be.

WHEN YOU AND I AS LEADERS CREATE THAT KIND OF VOLUNTEER CULTURE, WE CREATE A PLACE THAT MAKES SOMEONE FEEL APPRECIATED. GRATEFUL. VALUED. LOVED.

That's the kind of place we all want to come back to over and over again.

As leaders, we often want to make sweeping changes in our programs without first considering what kind of environment we are providing for those we serve.

No matter who you lead, no matter how big or small your volunteer team is, remember Dan's example, and aim to create a culture of people who will say YES to helping one another.

5. CELEBRATE SMALL STORIES

One of the really fun jobs you have as a leader is to make heroes out of your volunteers. Look for stories about the small things they've done that ended up making a bigger impact than they ever imagined.

TELL THEIR STORIES, EMAIL THEIR STORIES, AND CELEBRATE THEIR STORIES TO KEEP REMINDING VOLUNTEERS THAT IT IS THE SMALLEST OF THINGS THAT THEY DO THAT HAVE THE BIGGEST IMPACT.

Make them
the heroes of
your ministry:

A father decides to start coming to church because a volunteer hosted a dads and sons football game at his house.

A recently divorced mom with a two-year-old daughter loves coming to church because of a 66-year-old volunteer who greets them every week and walks them to their room. The little girl calls him her "Grandpa at the church."

One high school freshman named Mr. Michael is the reason two ADHD preschoolers come every week. He is the best one to keep them physically active while they are learning so they stay engaged and have fun. They come to see Michael.

One mom gives her middle school girls group small bottles of nail polish from the dollar store whenever they share how they acted on something they learned from the week before. Her girls have blown her away with their willingness to learn and grow.

IF YOU JUST SIMPLY LOOK AROUND, THESE STORIES ARE THERE.

They just take some time for you to find them. Put forth the effort, because when you do, it can make all of the difference in casting vision to volunteers who don't necessarily always see the fruits of their labor.

BE IT EVER SO HUMBLE . . . SMALL IS BIG.

TOP 10 THINGS
THAT SHOW VOLUNTEERS
BIG CARE

1. BECOME THEIR ADVOCATE
2. KEEP THEM INFORMED
3. ASK FOR THEIR OPINION
4. DON'T CUSS AT THEM
5. TELL THEM IT'S OK TO BE CRAZY (VALUE THEIR UNIQUENESS)
6. TELL THEM WHAT THEY ARE DOING RIGHT
7. MAKE SURE THEY HAVE FRIENDS
8. PRAY FOR THEM
9. EMPOWER THEM
10. LOVE THEM NO MATTER WHAT

CHAPTER 3

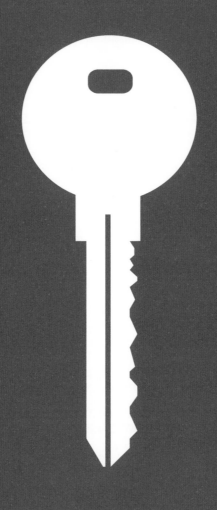

OWN, DON'T RENT

THE SCOOP

Owners know they will invest more, not less along the way, but get a bigger return on their investment. The day they sell their property, all of their hard work, sacrifice, and time will pay off. They end up getting more back in the end.

The same principle applies when you volunteer.

As a renter, you're planning to give the minimal amount of you . . . enough to check off the "giving back" box, but not enough to build great memories, make great friendships, or get your heart wrecked as you care about someone else.

If you just show up occasionally, you don't get to know anyone's story or see their life changed over time.

IF YOU SHOW UP THREE TIMES A YEAR, YOU WON'T IMPACT A CHILD'S FUTURE MUCH.

IF YOU SHOW UP ONCE A MONTH, IT WILL BE HARD TO BUILD SIGNIFICANT RELATIONSHIPS WITH KIDS OR TEENAGERS.

IF YOU SHOW UP ONLY DURING THE HOLIDAYS, YOU WILL MISS THE JOY THAT HAPPENS ALL YEAR LONG AND ONLY EXPERIENCE IT FOR A SEASON.

If you just stick your big toe in the water when it comes to helping someone else, you'll get one big toe's worth of life change.

Don't you want more than that? You're missing the best part! It's time to do something bigger, to invest more, and get a bigger return on your investment.

(WHAT WE TOLD YOUR VOLUNTEERS)

Renting is normal. Owning isn't. Well, okay, owning is normal for some people, but owning with a paid-off house, a clean lawn, and an impeccable record with the neighborhood isn't.

If you want to be a not normal volunteer, you need to be an owner, not a renter.

It's ironic that you start out as a volunteer worried about the time you may be losing in your busy schedule. Renting seems like a great option, because that way you won't lose too much. Your investment is small. But so is your return.

Quirky owners pray harder, work harder, and give more. They push to make a bigger investment in someone else's life. The more they do it, the more convinced they become over time. It's wisest to invest bigger in someone else's life, because there's simply so much for you to gain.

Owners aren't normal.

RUN WITH IT

(HOW YOU HELP YOUR VOLUNTEERS DO IT)

1. GET THE RIGHT PEOPLE IN THE RIGHT PLACE

We think there are a few ways to do this properly. First, you have to make sure you are honest with your new volunteers up front that the position they are in now will probably not be the position they end up in. When you start these conversations and volunteers understand that they are in an environment that is constantly changing, these conversations become a little easier.

Mention that most volunteers start somewhere that feels right to them at that time. But then many of them discover new things about themselves and want to try a different role. That is great! As a matter of fact, assure each volunteer that your goal is to help them find their best fit. This environment is open to them moving and changing what they like to do most, as long as we do the transition well along the way. We want each volunteer to soar under our leadership, and growing and changing comes along with the territory.

If you don't have these conversations, there is no questioning that people get attached to their volunteer positions. Have you ever been to a place where you meet someone who wears the same nametag they've had since 1973? You know, the kind somebody made with Chartpak rub-on letters?

You need to evaluate where your volunteers are on a consistent basis. If you are in a smaller organization, this can be done with your own eyes. However, as we talked about earlier, having a multi-tiered coaching structure in place is the best way for you to make this happen. You and your coaches need to constantly be observing, having conversations, and making sure your volunteers and their service roles are well-matched.

YOU CAN START TO IDENTIFY WHEN THINGS AREN'T A GOOD FIT WHEN YOU SEE . . .

VOLUNTEERS SHOWING UP LATE, OR NOT SHOWING UP AT ALL.

VOLUNTEERS WHO ARE DRAINED AT THE END OF THE TIME SLOT.

VOLUNTEERS WHO ARE CONSTANTLY COMPLAINING ABOUT THE TIME THEY HAVE SPENT SERVING.

If you see some of this, it is probably time to start shifting folks around. Start talking to them about what they like to do and what they think could improve in the areas where they serve.

But it's not always about seeing the negative.

When I (Adam) started volunteering, I was a small group leader for Kindergarten and first grade boys. They were a hoot! But after the first year, our children's director came up to me and said, "I'm not so sure you are in the right place." At first I was offended. How could she even say that to me? But she then said, "Your coach has been interacting with you and she thinks you have a great personality. Have you ever tried being on stage?" I hadn't, but I reluctantly agreed.

She was trying to get the best out of me and helped me develop talents I didn't even know I had.

2. ASK FOR WHAT YOU REALLY NEED

ONE OF THE WORST THINGS YOU CAN DO AS SOMEONE WHO LEADS VOLUNTEERS IS TO MAKE A MINIMAL ASK.

One of the temptations you might face as someone who leads volunteers is to make the same size ask of everyone. Sometimes we even give the impression that we just need "bodies in rooms" to fill ratios that somebody official put into their handbook. We think if you lead like that, you will end up with a lot of renters and very few owners.

We told you in Chapter One that we thought that you should not scare off your volunteers up front and that you should make the roles bite-size so everyone starts in a comfortable place. That is a good principle to apply as folks are just getting started.

But sometimes there are those unique people . . . those who have been around for a while or maybe those people who have known what is has been like to be an owner in another organization and they want to plug in right way. These individuals like difficult and challenging roles.

THEY ARE LOOKING FOR A LEADER WHO CAN PULL OUT THE BEST IN THEM.

I (Sue) had three men that fit this category. They were risk-takers in the market place. Business builders. Strategic problem-solvers. They had been serving in coach roles at the time, but they came to me wanting more. One of them said, "Sue, we're bored. You aren't asking enough of us."

I just stared at them in utter disbelief. Never had I heard anyone say those words to me before. I never imagined that I could be holding someone else back from serving. As we talked some more, I realized that they had a point.

They were challenging me to find ways to get more of their expertise into the game. And I took the challenge!

It wasn't like I didn't have tough problems on my desk that needed solutions. I needed all of the help I could get!

One of them took on our budget. He wanted to get us better deals on some of our supplies and save money. When I gave him an itemized copy of our budget, his face just lit up, totally jazzed about getting to work right then and there. He told me he could hardly drive home fast enough that night to put it all on spreadsheets.

Six months later, do you know how cool it was to have that man stand up and present our children's ministry budget to our executive board members? Boom! That was so awesome.

The other two men asked for my biggest recruiting challenge. I said the two-year-olds room. I was unable to get men to serve in that area. Their eyes got really big and they immediately started to brainstorm how they could solve it. The very next Sunday, there they both were, standing outside that room in the hallway, meeting and greeting every dad that walked by. They took some out for lunch and met some others for coffee during the week near where they worked downtown. I just stood and watched them take the hill with such confidence and relational skill. Months later, they were inside those rooms serving with the newbies they had recruited . . . six men. They rocked that room.

Then all three of them were ready for what was next. We were making a facility change at that time, so I put them on that project. Empowering them was fun for me and watching them fly higher and higher was pure delight. I learned tons from them.

I don't think I would have ever looked for these guys. Thankfully, they approached me and clued me in. I wouldn't have imagined that any volunteer would want to partner with me this way. But I underestimated how much they loved our vision. It rang their bell, and they wanted to play big not small. Maximally, not minimally. Hard, definitely not easy stuff.

YOU HAVE SOME OF THESE PEOPLE TOO. BE ON THE LOOKOUT FOR THEM.

They are waiting to dive into the deep end and can help you take your program to the next level. We make a mistake when we timidly only ask them to show up once a month.

There is a healthy tension here between giving someone an entry role and asking someone to serve every single week and to get involved at a higher level. That is where you as the leader come in. It is your responsibility to assess the situation and to evaluate where the volunteer is and then make the ask based on their personality, availability, and willingness to serve.

If the person and the fit is right, don't be afraid to make a big ask. Don't be afraid to tell them what the ministry or department needs. When you do, you might end up with some of the most influential owners you have ever seen.

3. GET OUT OF THEIR WAY

One day a small group leader came up to me (Adam) and said the following: "Hey, my boys and I are thinking about just going into the large group room and playing dodge ball after the Bible story rather than doing our small group activities today. Is that okay?" My response was one that most folks in charge of family programming would have: "You mean you are not going to use the color copies that we spent countless hours preparing today? And you are going to go blow off some steam and just 'hang out' today? Well, how thoughtful of you." (That was an internal response, way before the ministerial filter clicked into place.)

The external response was one that was a bit different. "Okay, we can go with that. But just this once because that time to discuss what you guys have just seen is really important."

So these fourth and fifth grade boys went into the open space and played dodge ball for about twenty minutes or so. They probably damaged some technical equipment to boot, but who's counting. They all came out sweaty, high five-ing each other, and looked to have had a great time.

THE MOST INTERESTING PART OF THIS STORY IS WHAT HAPPENED THE NEXT WEEK.

The next week the same small group leader came up to me and I am thinking, "Here we go again." I was surprised when he asked me for a stack of permission slips. I asked him what they were for and he said, "My boys and I had such a great time last week that we decided that we should all go to a movie together next month."

THIS GUY WAS AN OWNER.

If I had not gotten out of this guy's way, he never would have been able to build the connection he did and they would have never gone to a movie the next month. And who knows what is going to happen from there. Maybe a kid's life could be changed forever.

When we want too much control over something, it can get ugly.

Now don't get us wrong! We are not saying that any volunteer in any situation should have the ability to do whatever they want to. That would be madness.

BUT WE DO THINK, IN CERTAIN SITUATIONS, THERE SHOULD BE SOME WIGGLE ROOM FOR YOUR VOLUNTEERS TO BE ABLE TO DREAM WITHIN THE PARAMETERS OF THE VISION THAT YOU HAVE LAID OUT.

4. DEVELOP THEM

You have to train your volunteers. Period. This is a daunting statement for most leaders and we understand why. For most of us, when we hear the word training, fear trembles down our spine because there are two traits that are generally consistent in most training. Ready for them?

THEY ARE BORING.

and

NO ONE SHOWS UP.

Why would we even be interested in doing this then if this is the history behind these events? The reason we have to innovate is because developing volunteers is so essential. That's why we have to figure out new ways to train, new ways to deploy training resources, and new ways to consistently communicate information.

Here are three things you can give them.

Give them training events.

We hesitated to include this advice, but we do find that there is value in a physical rally-the-troops event where everyone comes together so that you can cast vision. Volunteers can look around and see that they aren't the only one in the department. There are others that care about the same cause that they do.

KEEP THEM SHORT. (Don't waste people's time. People are busy.)

KEEP THEM INFREQUENT. (People don't want to come to event after event. Do one as you kick off your school year and do one at the end of the year to celebrate.)

KEEP THEM MEANINGFUL. (Did we say that you shouldn't waste people's time? Make sure the information you are putting forward is inspirational, educational, meaningful, and short.)

KEEP THEM FUN. (And not typical church fun. Actually have fun. Figure out what your people like to do and infuse it into the event.)

Give them blogs and podcasts.

Find the best resources that you can to put directly into the hands of your people. Don't overdo it, because they might only have time to read one article or listen to one podcast. Instead, prioritize the ones that help take your ministry to the next level. Do some research yourself and then make a decision on how you want to deploy it with your volunteers.

MAYBE IT'S IN AN EMAIL.

MAYBE YOU GO OLD-SCHOOL AND PRINT AN ARTICLE IN A MEETING.

MAYBE YOU LISTEN TO A PODCAST FOR THREE WEEKS IN A ROW DURING A PRE-SERVICE MEETING.

Whatever deployment method works for you, get these things to your leaders. Even if they do listen only to that one podcast or read one article you give them, you still are making headway in casting vision that you want your volunteers to hear.

Give them snippets.

Create a Pinterest presence or a Twitter account for your volunteers to follow. Ask them all to follow it during your opening volunteer kickoff event and then tweet and pin leadership ideas, principles, and truths that you want your people to see.

This way it becomes a part of their everyday life.

Furthermore, ask them to favorite your account on these social media sites. That way they receive notifications when you post so it can end up popping up on their phone. Social media is going to be around for a while. Tap into it. Give them snippets of information; it might make the biggest difference. (Don't miss out on the opportunity to guide someone through these ideas like, "favoriting a page." You'll teach them a new skill, and a new funny verb at the same time.)

Try an individual approach.

Every volunteer appreciates a leader who wants to help them get better at what they are doing. It communicates thoughtfulness and belief in them. Very few people ever get this in their market-place job, so it's a welcome practice when you can offer it in a church setting.

Once a year go through your volunteers and coaches list and ask . . .

WHO NEEDS A GREAT BOOK?

WHO NEEDS A CONFERENCE?

WHO NEEDS TO VISIT ANOTHER LOCAL CHURCH TO LEARN FROM WHAT THEY ARE DOING?

WHO NEEDS TO BE RE-ENERGIZED BY A CREATIVE LIVE SHOW LOCALLY?

WHAT EXPERT COULD I BRING IN TO MEET WITH A FEW OF THEM?

WHO NEEDS A DIFFERENT ROLE?

WHO NEEDS TO TAKE A BREAK SO THEY DON'T BURN OUT?

WHO NEEDS TO SHADOW SOMEONE ELSE IN THE CHURCH TO LEARN HOW THEY DO THINGS?

This doesn't mean that every volunteer will take you up on your offer. But either way you win. Every volunteer will love that you thought of them, even if they say no.

For the ones who say yes, you let them know that you still want them to feel like they get more than they give in your organization.

5. ALLOW THEM A PLATFORM TO EXPRESS THEIR IDEAS

IF YOU ARE NEVER ACCESSIBLE TO YOUR VOLUNTEERS, THEY WILL SEE YOU AS DISTANT AND UNAPPROACHABLE.

If you are never in your office for them to say hi, never having coffee with them, and never hanging out outside of whatever arena you lead with your volunteers, you will have very little influence with them.

YOUR VOLUNTEERS HAVE IDEAS. AND THAT IS A GOOD THING.

Some leaders hear this and they run away hiding because sometimes ideas that volunteers have involve going back to the past. You may have heard a few of these . . .

> **"CAN WE BRING TABLES AND CHAIRS BACK TO THE ROOMS FOR SMALL GROUPS? THE CIRCLES AREN'T WORKING ANYMORE. WE NEED TO GO BACK TO ROWS."**

> **"IT'S TIME FOR US TO BRING BACK SOME CLASSICAL HYMNS FOR STUDENTS . . . YOU KNOW, THE STUFF I GREW UP WITH. IF WE ARE REALLY GOING TO TRAIN THEM WE NEED TO GET BACK TO OUR ROOTS."**

> **"DON'T YOU THINK WE SHOULD BE MAKING KIDS MEMORIZE THE WHOLE BIBLE INSTEAD OF JUST TALKING ABOUT HOW JESUS SAYS TO LIVE THEIR LIVES?"**

Yes, you will hear some of these ideas if you are accessible to your volunteers. Most people have fond memories of the experience they had growing up or when they came to faith. The truth is that times have changed, and most of you know that.

You will hear some ideas that you have to say no to. And saying no is a good thing. It gives you the opportunity to cast vision to your volunteers and say, "We can't do that because we are doing this. And 'this' is our end goal. So we have to prioritize." Those are awesome conversations where more vision casting occurs than you would ever think.

ON THE OTHER HAND, WHEN YOU ARE INTENTIONAL, VOLUNTEERS WILL ACTUALLY GIVE YOU SOME AWESOME IDEAS.

As our ministries grew, we needed some fresh ideas in order to get better at what we did. So, we asked our key coaches and leaders for their help. We were hungry for new ways of solving some challenges we kept running into over and over again.

We called this our Leadership Connection, and invited this group to come together once every three months for ninety minutes. To our great surprise, they came. And they jumped all of the way into our challenges. And they loved it.

HERE'S WHY . . .

We always provided an inexpensive dinner and gave them time to connect with each other relationally for thirty minutes. We were available as well, walking around and chatting with them. It was a great hang out time.

Then we got down to work. We introduced the problem of the night, and gave them 45 minutes to work in groups solving it. Watching them think hard, brainstorm, and challenge one another's ideas was cool. They took their role so seriously, and really came up with innovative solutions for us to try.

We asked each group to present their best ideas, and figured out how we could pilot some of them in one or two age levels to see what we could learn. The energy from this group was evident on those nights. Time just flew by, leaving us all wanting more.

The good news?

Most of their solutions were put into play permanently after the pilot, helping us improve how we served our families each year. Giving them all of the credit was our favorite part.

Side benefit? Talk about a way to develop owners! Talk about a way to grow leaders! We ended up hiring future staff members from the leaders in that gathering.

CHAPTER 4

YOU, ME, WE

THE SCOOP

This is not about me. It's not about you. It's about how WE do this together.

We've noticed that not normal volunteers work together differently than most.

It has to do with putting aside personal agendas and deciding to work on one bigger agenda that drew everyone together in the first place.

They know that something out of the ordinary happens whenever you get a group of people together who all have something in common. Something not at all normal.

There's a sense of camaraderie that emerges whenever . . .

YOU SIT IN THE STANDS WATCHING YOUR SPORTS TEAM PLAY.

YOU JOIN A CLUB.

A DISASTER HAPPENS IN YOUR TOWN.

YOU ATTEND A SUPPORT GROUP.

Whenever you find yourself with people who are experiencing the same thing you are, connection happens. No matter who you talk to, no matter if things are funny, sad, frustrating, or fantastic, you can identify with each other. You're all in the same boat. You are all sharing the same moment.

(WHAT WE TOLD YOUR VOLUNTEERS)

What started out as a normal "you" and "me" situation quickly turned into a not normal collective "we" experience. Some collective experiences last for an hour or two, some a couple of months or years, but others can last a lifetime.

Not normal volunteers want to give their best. They like doing whatever they are doing with class. That is one of the quality quirky things we admire so much about them: They show up prepared and ready to go. They come ready to play hard, with a work ethic that just can't be beat. They inspire us and everyone around them over and over again. And they make Heaven smile at their efforts.

Now it's your turn. You can do this, you can be part of a not normal team too. Your quirkiness just needs to grow a little.

RUN WITH IT

(HOW YOU HELP YOUR VOLUNTEERS DO IT)

1. BEGIN STRONG (WITH A KICKOFF)

For you to help your volunteers move from a "you" and "me" situation, you have to start your year with a bang.

The kickoff celebration for your school year is an essential part of you pumping them up to rock and roll their year into one big party!

The problem that we have seen with volunteer kickoffs is that they struggle to create momentum. Like we talked about earlier as it relates to training, most of them just aren't any good. They fail to create the momentum that they need to get the ball rolling, and they aren't much of a party at all. Lots of times they are planned by the wrong people. You want to assemble some party planners to help you think outside of the box. It doesn't have to be big. It just has to have energy and be fun.

Think about this:

YOUR KICKOFF EXPERIENCE WILL PAY OFF ALL YEAR LONG IF YOU DO IT RIGHT.

That means pulling the right team and theme together. Your kickoff event should be the event that other departments talk about, that people remember all year long, and that years from now those same people talk about when they remember the kickoff event that no one can forget. You're not only pumping up your volunteers for the first day in classroom or on a stage, you're giving them an ocean of inspiration they can draw from when times get tough or the year seems long.

Here's the good news.

KICKOFFS DON'T HAVE TO BE COMPLICATED.

KICKOFFS DON'T NEED LOTS OF TALKING HEADS.

KICKOFFS DON'T REQUIRE HUGE DOLLARS.

Feel better?

KICKOFFS DO NEED FOUR THINGS TO MAKE THEM EFFECTIVE:

Connection: The volunteers like to catch up relationally with each other. They want time to hang out and build relationships.

Fun: We are not talking the New York ball drop or anything like that, but this is where a theme sure helps. It's always easier for creative people to figure out what the fun should be once they know what the theme is. Don't forget to check out Pinterest . . . there are ideas galore on there about what others are doing to provide some fun moments. Even if you only have four volunteers, remember these same guidelines apply to you. Some of the best parties have a small group of friends having fun together.

Compelling vision: Come up with a way to get your merry band of volunteers excited once again about the mission you are all going to accomplish together. Remind them of what's at stake. Inspire them so they walk out sure about why they want to sign up to do this again.

Prayer: It's good to remember together that you have all of Heaven's help behind what you are doing. This keeps us from trying to take too much responsibility for what only God can really do. We just want to show up and do our part.

2. HAVE A HUDDLE

ONE OF THE MOST MEANINGFUL THINGS THAT VOLUNTEERS CAN DO IS SPEND TIME TOGETHER.

Generally, they aren't going to do that on their own so you are going to have to help them have a little bit of a kick-start. Whatever you call your time together, huddles are super-important to your ministry. We will just tell you a little bit of our experiences related to them.

You might think it would be difficult to get volunteers to attend. We say not true! Not when you do what we suggest on the next page. Not when you're not normal. When relationships are the priority of the meeting, we have seen attendance skyrocket.

WHEN YOU HAVE A SUCCESSFUL HUDDLE, YOUR MINISTRY WILL BE DIFFERENT. PERIOD.

Volunteers will begin to create that "You, Me & We" culture that we want them to create.

VOLUNTEERS WILL CONTINUE TO COME BACK TO SERVE BECAUSE THEY BELIEVE IN THE CAUSE THEY ARE SERVING.

VOLUNTEERS WILL COME BACK TO HONOR THE COMMITMENT THAT THEY MADE.

VOLUNTEERS WILL COME BACK BECAUSE THEY BELIEVE THEY ARE MAKING A DIFFERENCE IN THE LIVES OF KIDS OR TEENAGERS THAT THEY SERVE.

BUT, VOLUNTEERS WILL REALLY COME BACK OVER AND OVER AGAIN FOR THE COMMUNITY AND RELATIONSHIPS THEY HAVE WITH THE VOLUNTEERS THEY SERVE WITH.

Those relationships almost always begin in a huddle.

1

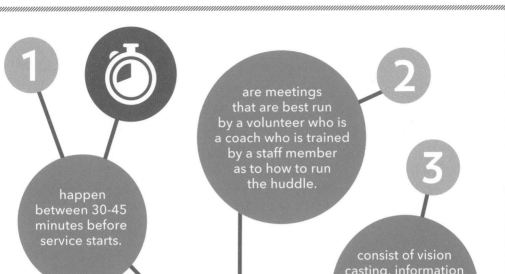

happen between 30-45 minutes before service starts.

2

are meetings that are best run by a volunteer who is a coach who is trained by a staff member as to how to run the huddle.

3

consist of vision casting, information sharing, curriculum adjustments, prayer requests, and overall fun.

HUDDLES:

must consist of doughnuts, bagels, coffee, and flavored coffee creamer. No exceptions.

generally consist of specific teams (Small Group Leaders, Greeters, Large Group, and the like). But look for times to bring the entire department of volunteers together.

should finish in time for volunteers to have at least 15 minutes to be in their designated spaces before anyone else arrives.

4

6

5

One of the sweetest stories we have ever seen in a huddle happened to a middle-aged single mother of two. She opened up one day and revealed in a huddle that she was going to need some time off from being a small group leader. She had reconciled with her ex-husband and they were expecting another child. Knowing what her fellow volunteers knew about her situation (which wasn't extremely healthy), they could have reacted in judgmental ways. But they did just the opposite. They rallied around this woman, prayed for her, supported her, and celebrated her. Her coach even asked, "When is the best date for this team to throw you a baby shower?"

THAT'S THE KIND OF "YOU, ME, & WE" WE ARE TALKING ABOUT. AND WHEN THINGS LIKE THIS HAPPEN, YOU CAN BUILD RELATIONSHIPS THAT WILL LAST A LIFETIME.

3. MID-YEAR INFUSION

So much of the time, volunteers serve in areas where no one says thanks.

BUSY PARENTS COLLECTING THEIR KIDS AFTER A SERVICE DON'T STOP TO SAY THANKS.

HIGH SCHOOL STUDENTS DON'T SAY THANKS FOR GIVING UP A YEAR OF SLEEP ON THEIR BEHALF.

MIDDLE SCHOOL STUDENTS ARE NONVERBAL AT THIS STAGE, SO NO THANKS THERE.

Not normal leaders are aware of this. We know that we can never give too much sincere appreciation to our volunteers.

Not normal leaders tweet about the set-up volunteers, appreciating those who quietly serve behind the scenes.

Not normal leaders actively look for ways to catch volunteers doing something awesome. They give specific thanks right then and there.

Not normal leaders write thank you notes.

Not normal leaders text great quotes to inspire volunteers.

Not normal leaders remind senior leaders to say thank you to volunteers from the main stage.

Not normal leaders Instagram the amazing work volunteers did to showcase and appreciate them.

Smart leaders make a really big deal about appreciating the small things that volunteers do all year long.

PICK A MONTH IN THE MIDDLE OF YOUR YEAR AND DECLARE IT VOLUNTEER APPRECIATION MONTH.

We like the midyear point, since that's the time when volunteer spirits seem to droop.

The year can start to feel forever long and ministry energy dips. It's the perfect time to give them a vision infusion, to jump-start their engines. Crank up their performance, because they are making a huge difference.

NOW, FIGURE OUT WAYS TO CONVINCE THEM OF THAT DIFFERENCE THEY'RE MAKING.

Put up banners. Add streamers somewhere where they will see them. Pick one table and decorate that one to the nines for the month. Bring the party to them. Rent a red carpet for a small area that they can walk down. Ask someone in your town to donate some free cupcakes that say "THANKS" or see if a moms small group would bake some for you. Maybe some dads would grill hot dogs one week so that volunteers and their families could stay and eat for free after they serve.

Be creative and use whatever you have at your disposal. Each week of that month, surprise your volunteers in four different small ways.

Ask some key parents to email you some notes that you can read to them. Make some of these serious and some of them funny. Volunteers love to laugh and cry over these.

Have a parent make a video and tell how their family has been impacted by these volunteers.

HOWEVER YOU DO IT, YOUR VOLUNTEERS WILL FEEL HONORED THAT YOU DID THIS TO SERVE THEM. ACTIONS DO SPEAK LOUDER THAN WORDS, AND THESE FOUR WEEKS SCREAM "VOLUNTEERS MATTER HERE."

That's why it's important, as you create a "You, Me & We" type of mentality, to give your department a shot of energy during the middle of the year to keep the momentum going. Depending on your ministry, it might need to be even more frequent.

4. NAVIGATE CONFLICT

People are people. Even Christians. Even those people who are followers of the "love your neighbor as yourself'" movement can still have drama among themselves sometimes.

And even though these people might be good people, they don't always get along.

Fact:
Volunteers, when working together, will have conflict. It arises in situations you least expect.

We've heard of . . .

VOCALISTS BATTLING FOR THE SPOTLIGHT ON THE STAGE WHILE SINGING WORSHIP SONGS WITH KIDS.

COFFEE VOLUNTEERS ARGUING OVER WHICH STATION THEY ARE SUPPOSED TO BE PLACED AT.

SMALL GROUP LEADERS WHO SHARE THE SAME ROOM ARGUING OVER NOISE LEVEL.

And just wait until you have a husband and wife serving together and they decide to get divorced.

Think that can interrupt the "You, Me, & We" mentality? You bet it can!

Navigating conflict can be one of the most difficult parts of your job as a leader of people who work for you for free, but that's where you come in. When this is handled properly, it can help bring volunteers closer together and can promote the type of bonding that we want to happen with volunteers.

One Sunday, while I (Sue) was acting producer in the back of the room next to a very simple soundboard, I got a huge wake up call. I asked for the sound to be turned up on Jamie's microphone. She was one of the four worship singers up front that day and I could not hear her at all. The guy at the soundboard leaned over to me and whispered, "Sue, I can't. Her mic is off for a reason. She can't sing."

WHAAAAAAAAAAATTTTTTT?

After the program was over, I sat down with the three programming volunteers to hear the rest of the story. Turns out that Jamie had been on the worship team for years and no one ever wanted to tell her that singing was not in her wheelhouse. So the audio guy just turned her mic off whenever she was up front with the others, and she was never the wiser.

I asked why they thought this was a more loving thing to do for Jamie?

The reply? "She's just such a nice lady; we didn't want to hurt her feelings."

EVER BEEN IN A SITUATION LIKE THAT?

Do you remember this verse from Ephesians 4:15? **Speak the truth in love.** This principle helps us honor our relationships authentically with one another, but realistically speaking, it's a highly underused practice. Let's apply this passage principle here, and see what we can learn about navigating conflict together.

SPEAK

The truth is, most of us get stuck right here. Right out of the gate. No one likes to confront a troublesome situation or person and "speak." That makes us uncomfortable. We don't want to initiate a conversation and "speak" because we're afraid of what the reaction might be. What on earth would we even say?

So, we do our very best to avoid speaking. We prefer to stick our heads in the sand and wait it out, hoping the whole thing will just blow over. But in our experience, way too often these things just blow up, not over. And volunteers get disillusioned in the aftermath of the explosion.

HERE'S WHY THAT DOESN'T WORK.

When we let conflict fester, volunteers end up serving in a toxic environment. The people who surround them may have a laundry list against you or someone else, and eventually that overflows. All of that gets shared where it doesn't belong. In this scenario, everyone loses. The new volunteer gets a bad first impression. Who wants to join a team of people that are "mad" over a bunch of stuff? The regular volunteers long for someone to fix the problem so everyone can move on. They didn't sign up for this kind of drama. The kids and students who inevitably overhear the complaining from volunteers see unauthentic faith being lived out by the very people telling them how to grow a real faith.

God has a better way to navigate conflict, and it starts with initiating a conversation. Somebody needs to initiate and get the ball rolling. Someone has to speak.

I made a phone call to Jamie that night and scheduled a time to meet her for coffee after she got off of work one night that week.

THE TRUTH

Are you familiar with the phrase, "The truth hurts"?

Here's what you need to remember: the truth can definitely be hard to hear. But finding out the truth through the back door or that you have been deceived hurts way more.

As a leader,
I would rather have a
volunteer come to me
and tell the truth about
something I did or
said, so I can make
it right with them
immediately.

I know that I am an imperfect leader and don't want to pretend otherwise. My volunteers have strengthened me so much by telling me the truth over the years. It gives me a chance to apologize to them, ask for forgiveness, and make progress. My promise to them is that I will try not to make the same mistake twice.

I WANT TO LEARN AND GET BETTER EVERY SINGLE YEAR. THEY DESERVE THAT.

In Jamie's case, I first had to tell her the truth. I had to say that because people didn't want to hurt her feelings, they had given her inaccurate feedback on her areas of strength. They wanted what was best for her, but didn't know how to tell her that she was in the wrong spot. I told her that I was so sorry this happened, and that I wanted to make it right.

She cried. Big crocodile tears. I felt awful.

After a few more minutes went by, I told her that there was now a new opportunity in front of her. She would be able to find out what she was really great at, and put that strength to use for Kingdom impact. I told her we would figure that out together, if she were open to the idea. I asked her to pray about it, and I would check in with her later in the week to see how she was feeling about everything.

IN LOVE

So much about speaking the truth has to do with how you say what you say. Be gentle. Don't yell. Let your anger subside before you approach the other person. Don't make this a fly-by hallway conversation where you have to rush through what you need to say. Pick the right time and place. Patiently walk through what happened.

Remember your goal in all of this is restoration. You want to restore your relationship with this person. Your goal is not to win. Your goal is not to always be right.

Own what you did wrong. What part did you play? What could you have done better?

Follow up afterward to make sure everything is okay. When I called Jamie and asked whether she wanted to meet and talk about exploring next steps, she said yes.

I was prepared for this to go either way.

But you know why she stayed?

Because she really believed in our vision and what we were doing together. She decided to give us another chance to make a fan out of her. We obviously had a long way to go.

THERE WILL BE TIMES THAT YOU HAVE TO NAVIGATE CONFLICT.

You don't have to be an expert at it because you aren't a counselor (even though you might feel like it at times). You just have to work your way through it enough that you can keep everyone on the same page. Which also isn't the easiest thing to do! But you're a leader. You've got this!

5. END CELEBRATING

WHAT GOOD IS A YEAR'S WORTH OF HARD WORK
WITHOUT A CELEBRATION AT THE END?

If you are giving your volunteers who serve every week the summer off (see chapter 7), then you want to send them out with a celebration. Furthermore, you want them to commit to volunteering again before you send them away.

Your year-end celebration gathering needs to happen every year and needs to be a party. It needs to be something that your volunteers can't wait to come to and you need to use it to your advantage.

This is a time where you can . . .

SAY THANK YOU.

SHARE FUNNY STORIES.

REMIND THEM OF THE DIFFERENCE THEY HAVE MADE.

It is also a great time to bring in the senior leader of your organization to hang out with your volunteers and express his or her gratitude.

This isn't just a "pop in" appearance by this individual. He or she should stay for the entire event and hang out with these people who have given of themselves in a way that most people will never do.

THE COOL THING ABOUT THIS EVENT IS AS MUCH AS IT NEEDS TO BE PROGRAMMED, IT CAN ALSO BE CHILL AND RELAXED. IT CAN BE A TIME OF HANGING OUT.

Our advice to you:

WALK AROUND SLOWLY, AVAILABLE TO JUST HANG OUT.

GET TO KNOW A VOLUNTEER WHO YOU DON'T KNOW VERY WELL.

STOP AND SPEND A FEW MOMENTS WITH ONE OF YOUR MOST INFLUENTIAL COACHES.

DON'T GET SO WRAPPED UP IN THE PLANNING OF THIS EVENT THAT YOU MISS THIS EVENT.

Then you should talk. You should get up and say a few words to your people, these ones who have given back to their church and their community. After all, they have also given back to you. They have trusted you, followed you, and served you and the vision you set forth. Thank them for it. Tell them how much it means to you that they have stood by you through the thick and the thin.

MAKE THIS MOMENT MEAN SOMETHING BECAUSE YOU ONLY GET IT ONCE A YEAR.

At the end of your event, talk about the future. Talk about when you will begin the next year.

(And have your kickoff date ready to go so the people who are celebrating the end of one year can have the next one ready to go on their calendar.)

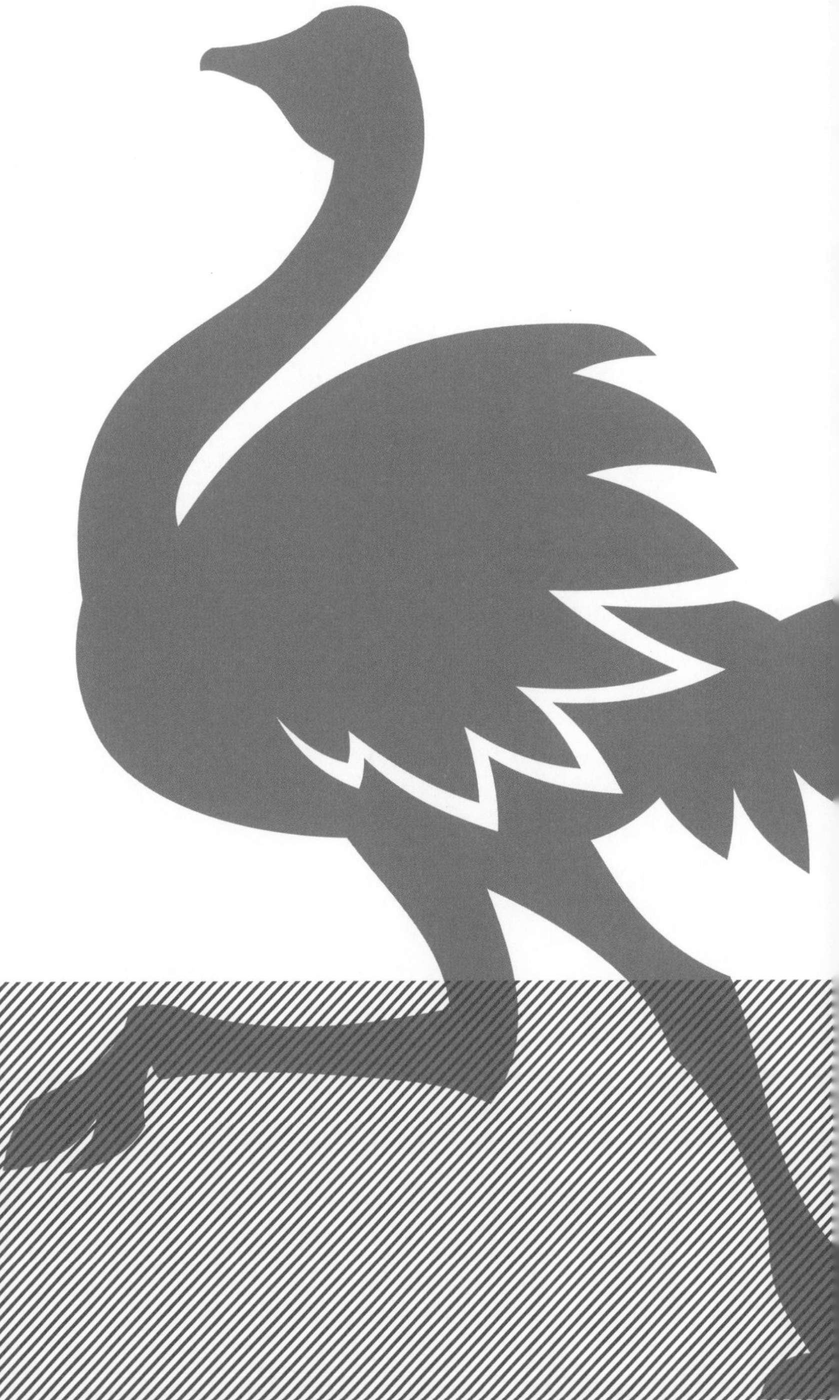

CHAPTER 5

HONOR THE LEADER

THE SCOOP

If you are a part of something where you don't embrace the vision, get out of it!

Your job as a volunteer is not to change the vision of a program that you are involved in. Your job is to support it, and hopefully that's what attracted you to the opportunity in the first place.

It will absolutely drain you to be a part of a vision you do not support.

YOU WILL WANT TO QUIT.

YOU WILL GO HOME EXHAUSTED.

YOU WILL THINK ABOUT WAYS TO CHANGE THIS TO BE SOMETHING YOU WANT IT TO BE.

When you support the vision a leadership group has set forth, it is like you are a part of a team. You are rallying around this vision with a cadre of people who believe in it too. It is so fun to be a part of.

Sometimes the best thing that a volunteer can do is amicably move on if they are in conflict with their leader over vision.

Allow us to be blunt: we need you. We need volunteers.

WE NEED YOU TO PRAY FOR US.

WE NEED YOU TO LOVE US.

(WHAT WE TOLD YOUR VOLUNTEERS)

WE NEED YOU TO SUPPORT US.

WE NEED YOU TO HONOR AND EMBRACE THE VISION GOD HAS GIVEN US.

AND SOMETIMES WE NEED YOU TO PROVIDE US PRESCRIPTION MEDICATION. (WE'RE KIDDING ABOUT THAT. RIGHT?)

This can happen in big ways and little ways. They can range from as small as not complaining about the types of pencils that they picked out to as big as saying "Yes" to the vision they have for the church and local community. It could be as small as pretending you like the new carpet that was picked out to as big as standing next to your leader when someone else tries to take him or her down.

It is so important that volunteers stand next to their leader during good and difficult times. It makes a world of difference. That might be the most not normal thing that you can do as you serve. We know we say that a lot in this book – but that's because we really mean it.

RUN WITH IT

(HOW YOU HELP YOUR VOLUNTEERS DO IT)

1. MODEL IT (BY HONORING THE LEADERS ABOVE YOU)

LET'S BE HONEST WITH EACH OTHER FOR A SECOND: EVERYONE HAS SOMEONE THAT THEY REPORT TO.

If you are reading this book right now, you have a boss. There are leaders in place above you who tell you what to do, set a vision, and help steer the ship from a macro level. The truth is, if you want your volunteers to honor you, you need to model it by honoring the leaders who are in authority over you.

Don't get us wrong. Things are frustrating sometimes, especially in ministry. If you are frustrated, you should have a sounding board where you can air some of your frustrations. But that sounding board should never be your volunteers (and it probably shouldn't be your spouse, either. But we will save that discussion for another time).

Maybe you are struggling modeling this right now because, just like some of your volunteers, you are a part of a vision that you do not support. This could be something short-term, something you'll get through, something you kind of expect because it goes with the territory in every job everywhere. The way you put on your game face and lead well anyway will be an example to everyone who will one day need to put on their game face for you.

EVERY LEADER HAS A BAD DAY, SOMETIMES EVEN A BAD SEASON, BUT EVERYTHING GETS BETTER.

Remember the big vision. Overlook the small slights. Do what you can to find people who will point out the better even in bad times. After all, playing well with others still counts even when you get way past third grade.

We also realize it may be more than that. Maybe there is a leader above you that you can no longer follow or support.

Allow us to tell you what we told your volunteers.

SOMETIMES THE BEST THING A LEADER CAN DO IS AMICABLY MOVE ON IF THEY ARE IN CONFLICT WITH THEIR LEADER OVER VISION.

It will drain you as a leader. It's not fair for you, and it's not fair for your leader. And your volunteers will be able to tell.

THEY ARE SMART.

THEY KNOW WHEN PEOPLE AREN'T ALL IN.

THEY CAN TELL WHEN THE TIME IS UP.

It is a tough pill to swallow if you are here. But it might just be for the best. This way you can get into an environment where you fully embrace vision and respect leaders above you and that can trickle down all the way to how your volunteers treat you.

2. BE A LEADER WORTH HONORING (AND ADMIT WHEN YOU ARE WRONG)

WE WISH THAT WE COULD SLIP EVERY LEADER ON THE PLANET A GLASS OF "HUMILITY JUICE" EVERY NOW AND THEN.

(They don't make it. Some of our volunteers have tried to find it for us. Especially for Adam.) For whatever reason, as leaders grow, a lot of them have trouble admitting when they are wrong. Every one of us has been wrong before. It is just a part of life. We will never get every decision right.

What makes a leader worth honoring is when their volunteers see them own up to a mistake they've made.

There is no way that leaders will . . .

HAVE GREAT IDEAS 100 PERCENT OF THE TIME.

GET EVERY DECISION RIGHT.

RESPOND CORRECTLY IN EVERY CONVERSATION.

THIS IS WHY WE HAVE TO ADMIT WHEN WE MESS UP A LITTLE OR A LOT.

There was this crazy idea that I (Adam) had when I was at a church in Michigan. I had an idea to do a pet show for families in the church parking lot. It sounded good on paper until the day of the show. Not only did very few people show up, but those who did show up showed up with dogs . . . multiple dogs, big dogs, little dogs, friendly dogs, mean dogs, overly friendly dogs, dogs and more dogs. And did I mention these dogs did not like each other? Some fought in the parking lot, there was endless barking, and we couldn't even hold the "best in show" competition because there was so much noise from dogs going insane.

To make it worse, I forgot to put someone on duty to pick up all of the "leftover," if you get my drift. By the end of the event, we had an empty parking lot full of dog poop.

THE EVENT DID NOT GO WELL, AND EVERYONE KNEW IT.

I had to go back to my team and say, "Guys, this one was a miss on my part. Never again." Had I gone back to them and defended the idea even after it tanked, they would have looked at me like I belonged in an animal asylum.

Leaders, if you want to be a leader worth honoring, sometimes you have to get vulnerable and open up when you don't get everything just right.

YOUR VOLUNTEERS WILL RESPECT YOU FOR IT AND HONOR YOU IN A VERY DIFFERENT WAY.

3. BE A LEADER WHO BUILDS OTHERS UP

When coaching a leader this past year, we discovered that not building others up was his greatest weakness. And it was costing him dearly.

HE WAS SUPER-ORGANIZED.

HE WAS A GOOD COMMUNICATOR.

HE HAD A GREAT VISION FOR THE FUTURE.

But his volunteers felt he was too much of a perfectionist. They felt like they never did anything well enough to satisfy his standard of excellence. He was always pushing them to work harder, prepare more, constantly striving to make more progress more quickly.

THE RESULT?

Volunteers began to walk away, anxious to put distance between this leader and themselves. It's hard to stay engaged under a leader that makes you feel like you are always failing.

THE REMEDY?

Determine as a leader to use words that build others up all around you.

Think about this for a second. Isn't it true that leaders who are positive and encouraging to others are the ones that people like to be around? Who doesn't like to hear someone tell them they just did a good job?

Here's what we need to keep in mind. Encouragement is essential for developing volunteers. They want to be coached by a leader that truthfully points out the things they are doing right. You can still give them feedback on where they can improve, but give that in small, strategic doses. (Remember, "Speak the truth in love.") Don't forget many volunteers are trying brand new skills, so give them a safe place emotionally to start.

> Keep verbally pointing out to volunteers how far they've come, not harping on how far they still have to go.

This will help them want to keep trying for the right reasons. This will give them the sense that they can do this. All volunteers want to feel like they are winning at what they are doing.

VOLUNTEERS WILL HAVE AN EASIER TIME RESPECTING AND HONORING A LEADER WHO USES THEIR WORDS TO BUILD OTHERS UP.

4. BE ALL IN

If you are asking your volunteers to be owners and not renters, then you better be one yourself. If you want them to honor you, you better be in the trenches with them.

A good rule of thumb is to remember that whatever you want your volunteers to do, you must do first. They take their cue from you.

Leaders always
lead the way and
set the standard for
everyone else.

IF YOU WANT YOUR TEAM TO BE PASSIONATE, THEN YOU BE PASSIONATE FIRST.

IF YOU WANT YOUR VOLUNTEERS TO SERVE OTHERS, THEN YOU NEED TO SERVE OTHERS FIRST.

IF YOU WANT A TEAM WITH A GREAT ATTITUDE, THEN YOU BETTER HAVE ONE FIRST.

Volunteers love to hear what leaders have to say, but they make their decision to follow based on what a leader does.

ACTIONS ALWAYS SPEAK LOUDER THAN WORDS.

We were called in to consult with a medium-sized church that had just lost their previous leader. The children's ministry had been losing volunteers for the last couple of years, but now the entire thing had imploded. Everyone in senior leadership was wondering what went wrong.

The only ones who could tell us the answers to their question were the volunteers. There weren't any other full-time staff members, just a couple of hourly administrators bravely trying to hold weekends together.

We asked to have a meeting with all volunteers past and present. This was going to be an open dialogue about what kind of leader we needed to find in order to create the best children's ministry in this church.

The room was full when the meeting started. About forty people showed up. We asked them to tell their name, where they had served, and one of the best things that had happened to them when they were serving here.

These volunteers were incredible. They were open about their best experiences, telling stories that brought tears more than once to everyone in the room. We could not have loved them more after hearing their heart for the kids they had been serving.

We asked them what they thought was holding this ministry back from becoming all it could be?

Big silence.

Okay, we tried asking a different question.

What kind of leader would be able to inspire you to jump back into this ministry?

That's when the whole room came alive, anxious to weigh into this discussion.

We started making a list of their answers:

> **SOMEONE WHO WILL DO WHAT THEY SAY THEY WILL DO.**
>
> **ONE WHO WILL COME IN EARLY AND STAY LATE.**
>
> **SOMEONE WHO WILL JUMP IN AND HELP US.**
>
> **A LEADER THAT ENERGIZES OTHERS.**
>
> **A LEADER WHO MAKES OTHERS LOOK GOOD.**
>
> **SOMEONE WHO WILL GO TO BAT FOR US.**
>
> **A LEADER WHO RETURNS PHONE CALLS.**

THEY WERE SAYING THAT THEY WANTED A LEADER WHO WAS ALL IN. THEY WANTED SOMEONE WHO OWNED THE MINISTRY WITH THEM.

A volunteer who was engaged in this conversation started praying about this position. Months later, she became the next leader. And she jumped ALL IN right from the start.

When volunteers have that kind of leader, they get excited about trying to do the impossible with God's help, pushing ministry limits for Kingdom good in ways they never thought possible before.

5. STAND UP FOR YOURSELF

We have found that in certain circumstances, leaders can be doormats to their volunteers. This is especially true for younger leaders with volunteers who have been tenured for a decent length of time. This won't help your volunteers "honor the leader." Over time, they could begin to look at you as someone who doesn't have a backbone or someone who won't stand up for the vision.

Let's face it, if you work at a church and are leading volunteers, you are bound to run into volunteers who . . .

ARE RELATED TO THE SENIOR PASTOR.

SERVE ON THE DEACON BOARD

HAVE BEEN AROUND FOR THIRTY YEARS, WHICH IS A LOT LONGER THAN YOU HAVE.

Historically some these people (and don't get us wrong . . . not ALL of these people) have used their influence to get what they want.

And who wants to stand up to these people? They have a lot of influence.

We have heard countless stories of leaders being hauled into the senior pastor's office or a board meeting after being tattled on by someone who has influence.

Rather than fight against these people and create an internal war at your church, maybe it is time to invest some of your time with these key influencers and ask them to stand beside you rather than against you.

THERE IS TENSION THERE, AND YOU ARE THE ONE WHO HAS TO MANAGE IT.

The fact of the matter is that if you let people run roughshod over your good name and abuse you, you won't get the proper respect that you deserve.

(On the other hand, don't forget about that honoring your elders part so make sure you stand up for yourself in the right way. This advice isn't a license to be disrespectful to the people who have put in the hard work before you. "Elder" has almost the same letters as "leader" and there's something about them in the Bible. But you get our point.)

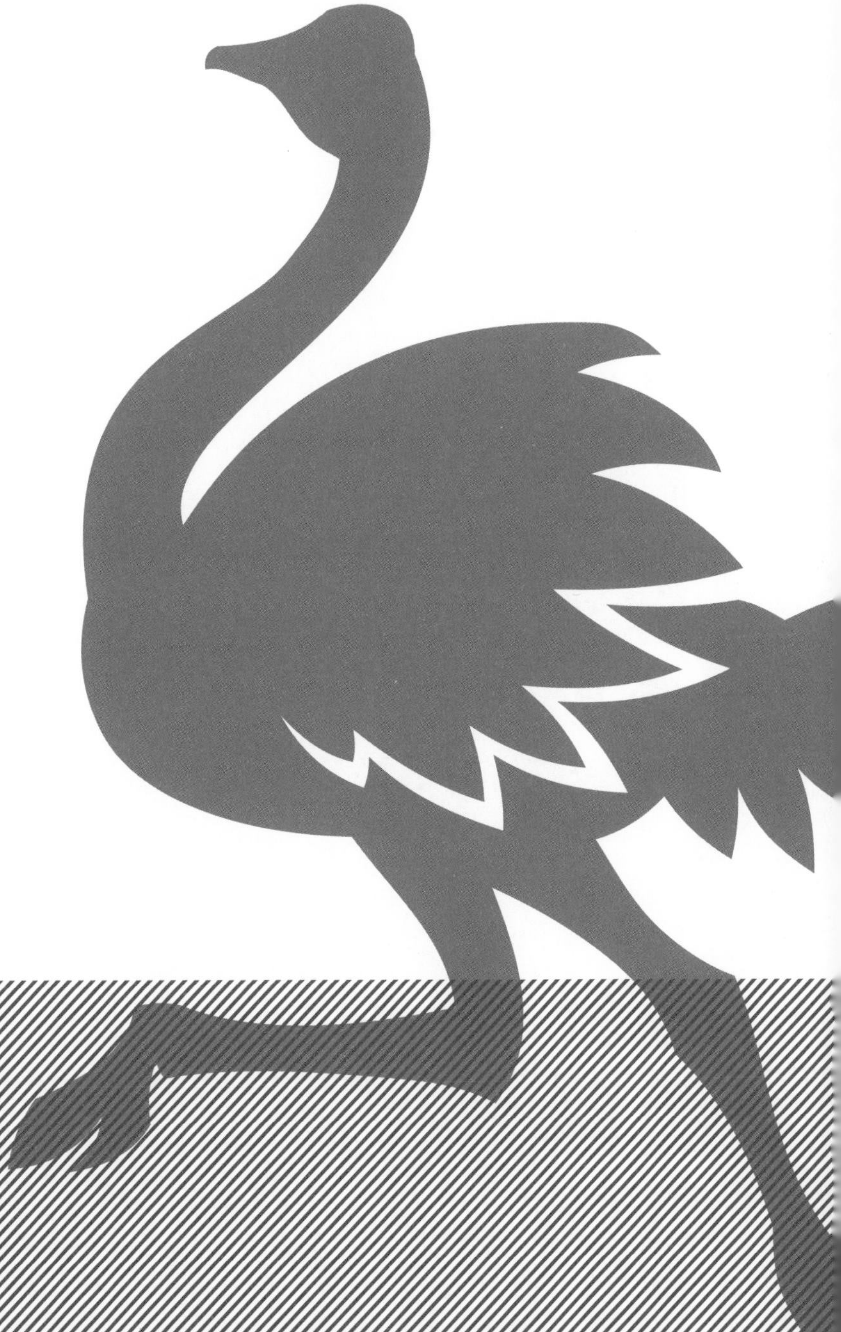

CHAPTER 6

REPLACE YOURSELF

THE SCOOP

 Believe it or not, there will come a day when you feel like you've found your zone. You are hitting your stride, feeling comfortable, like you've finally gotten your arms wrapped around this thing that you're doing.

And then . . .

A NEW OPPORTUNITY OPENS UP FOR YOU.

ANOTHER VOLUNTEER WANTS TO DO WHAT YOU ARE DOING.

SOMEONE COMES ALONG WHO CAN DO THIS BETTER THAN YOU.

THE GROWTH OF YOUR CAUSE GETS BIGGER AND YOU NEED MORE RECRUITS.

WHAT DOES A NOT NORMAL VOLUNTEER NEED TO DO?

Replace yourself.

This topic is personal, deep, and can press us to examine what is going on inside of our own heart and mind.

You probably never ever imagined having this discussion when you walked into your volunteering spot that first day, did you?

Especially after we've just spent the first five chapters telling you how important it is to start volunteering, own what you

(WHAT WE TOLD YOUR VOLUNTEERS)

do and don't rent what you do, honor the leader, and more, and now we're telling you to move on? Kind of, yes.

Allow us to explain before you deposit this book in the nearest trash receptacle.

Think back over all of the jobs you have had throughout your life. It could be when you were in high school and you were flipping burgers, or it could be your first executive position with a corporation. This truth is true about each and every job: someone else is doing that job now.

And as much as you love what you are doing now at your church, you innately realize you won't be doing it forever. Change is something all of us can count on happening, and it will happen to you as a volunteer as well. And it's a good thing, because change helps us keep growing into the "what's next" in our future.

You are where you are now for a time and a season, but what you are a part of is bigger than you and your service. Somewhere up ahead, when the time is right, your next quirky step will be to move on to something else and allow someone new to do what you are doing now. (And they might even be better at it!)

We said this would be difficult.

RUN WITH IT

(HOW YOU HELP YOUR VOLUNTEERS DO IT)

1. PLAN TO GROW

Once you start having success in recruiting, training, and growing volunteers, more and more will show up and want to be a part of the program you are creating. Trust us . . . it happens. The problem is that so many of us are treading water just to get a body into a room that we don't plan for growth related to volunteers. We might plan for growth as it relates to kids or teenagers or space, but most of us have no plan as it relates to accommodating the growing numbers of volunteers we will have.

Moreover, if we put a plan in place (we will talk about that next) for volunteers to replace themselves, we need to be set up for growth.

YOU MIGHT BEGIN TO ASK YOURSELF THESE QUESTIONS:

WHEN MY VOLUNTEERS REPLACE THEMSELVES, WHERE DO THEY GO ONCE THEY ARE REPLACED?

WHAT HAPPENS WHEN VOLUNTEERS ARE BEATING DOWN THE DOORS TO GET INVOLVED BUT OUR POSITIONS ARE ALL FILLED UP?

WHERE DO I LEAD PEOPLE WHO WANT TO MOVE FROM ONE POSITION TO THE NEXT BECAUSE THEY MIGHT NOT BE IN THE EXACT RIGHT SPOT?

Most of us do not have a good answer for any of the above questions. And that is a normal kind of response. But if you are going to be the kind of not normal leader who is leading not normal volunteers, you better be ready for this one.

Here are two small tips that might help you help your volunteers with implementing this idea of replacing themselves.

1. YOU SHOULD PLAN FOR EXPANSION.

We both served in ministries that were focused on strategic expansion. We created positions for everything that we could think of. We had bouncers, copy makers, we doubled up greeters, a cleanup crew, and more. You name it. We had it. Because we never wanted to turn away someone who was a new volunteer, or someone who wanted to replace themselves.

Momentum, and numbers of volunteers, grew rapidly with this strategy.

2. YOU SHOULD STRATEGICALLY MEET WITH VOLUNTEERS WHO REPLACE THEMSELVES.

See, some of our volunteers get confused with the idea of replacement. When you replace yourself it doesn't mean that you are done with volunteering. It just means you move onto something better. Something you might be more suited for related to the stage of life that you are in. If you aren't the one guiding this process from a leadership perspective, you might end up losing some of your best volunteers along the way. Encourage them that when they replace themselves it isn't the end, it is only the beginning.

2. ENCOURAGE APPRENTICING

We talked earlier about how to make volunteers owners and not renters, but just because we are leading them there it doesn't mean that they have the ability to do whatever they want when replacing themselves.

A SYSTEM NEEDS TO BE IN PLACE TO GUIDE VOLUNTEERS THROUGH THIS PROCESS.

Allow us to give you an example:

It would not be a good idea—let us take that a step further, it would be an extremely poor idea—for a long-term small group leader with a group of third grade girls to suddenly proclaim that she understands the idea of replacing herself and bring in a new leader and then abandon the group. Cold turkey.

What is wrong with that you might ask? She replaced herself. Well, yes, she did. But it wasn't done properly. For certain volunteer positions and in certain scenarios, a very careful and meticulous vetting process will help make sure the volunteer you are replacing yourself with is the right fit . . . for the program, and the group of individuals.

IT'S PROBABLY A LOT DIFFERENT FOR A DOOR GREETER THAN IT IS A SMALL GROUP LEADER OR A LEAD VOCALIST, BUT THE PRINCIPLE REMAINS THE SAME.

It takes some time . . .

TO UNDERSTAND THE DEPARTMENT.

TO GET ACQUAINTED.

TO GET TO KNOW THOSE YOU ARE SERVING WITH.

TO MAKE SURE IT IS THE RIGHT FIT.

REMEMBER, IF YOU DON'T HAVE THE RIGHT PEOPLE IN THE RIGHT PLACE, EVERYONE WILL SUFFER AND THEN ALL THAT "REPLACING YOURSELF" BENEFIT WILL HAVE BEEN LOST.

This is why we recommend an apprenticing system for your program, for small positions and really big positions.

Apprenticing systems sometimes consist of a very detailed process, but having volunteers who understand replacing themselves will make this more organic in your ministry. They are the people who usually find the apprentices and bring them to you as you consider whether they should begin the process.

That is our job.
To train our current
volunteers to understand
the vision, and then
they go find
the people.

HERE IS WHAT A GOOD APPRENTICING SYSTEM LOOKS LIKE:

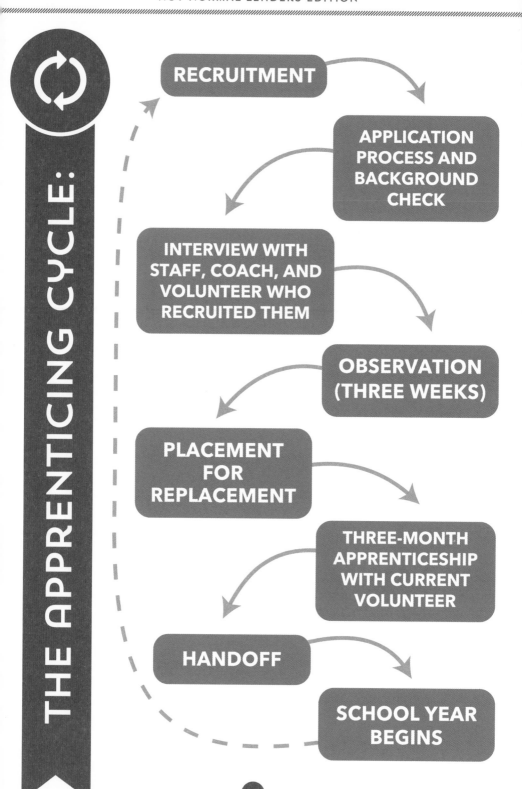

THE APPRENTICING CYCLE:

RECRUITMENT

APPLICATION PROCESS AND BACKGROUND CHECK

INTERVIEW WITH STAFF, COACH, AND VOLUNTEER WHO RECRUITED THEM

OBSERVATION (THREE WEEKS)

PLACEMENT FOR REPLACEMENT

THREE-MONTH APPRENTICESHIP WITH CURRENT VOLUNTEER

HANDOFF

SCHOOL YEAR BEGINS

3. VOLUNTEERING IS AND ISN'T SEASONAL

We fully believe that volunteering is not a seasonal thing. Volunteers should plug in as consistently as they can for as long as they can.

BUT SOMETIMES VOLUNTEERS NEED A SEASON IN THEIR LIFE TO RECHARGE THEIR BATTERIES.

There was a volunteer we heard about who was a small group coach. Her name is Kathy. Kathy was on the ground floor of training small group leaders and she had been a coach since the beginning of the program. For seven years, she had been serving every week and leaning into those who led kids. The great part about Kathy was that she understood that every week didn't just mean every week. She was the kind of leader whose role was not just limited to Sunday. She invested in her team and their personal lives. Then, one day she came up to the leader of her program and said, "I just want you to hear it from me, I'm replacing myself."

YOU CAN IMAGINE THE REACTION OF A LEADER TO LOSE SUCH A KEY VOLUNTEER.

It was a bit of a shock. But then Kathy said something that blew this leader's mind. She said, "But, I'm only replacing myself for a season. I will be back in two years. You have to understand. Two of my kids are having children this year and I am needed at home, and this is just a season. I'll be back."

You can imagine what this leader was thinking, "Yeah, right. You'll be back . . . " But the fact is, Kathy came back. To her exact position that she left and she is still serving to this day.

We tell you this story because it is important for you to know that some of your volunteers go through seasons in their lives where they need a break.

And a break can be a very good thing.

A break can be the thing that they need to reorient themselves and come back stronger than ever.

SO . . .

DON'T TAKE THAT PERSONALLY.

BE GRACIOUS IN YOUR UNDERSTANDING.

TAKE THEM AT THEIR WORD (EVEN IF SOME NEVER COME BACK).

AND WISH THEM THE ABSOLUTE BEST FOR THE SEASON OF LIFE THEY MIGHT BE IN.

4. UNDERSTAND IT'S EMOTIONAL

This all sounds easy doesn't it? Replacing yourself. It seems easy to us—and then you actually do it.

Think about some of your most seasoned volunteers who have been in the game for a long time.

MAYBE SOMEONE HAS ROCKED BABIES FOR ALMOST TWENTY YEARS.

MAYBE A SMALL GROUP LEADER HAS HAD THE SAME GROUP OF KIDS FOR SIX YEARS AND IS READY TO HAND THEM OFF.

MAYBE VOLUNTEERS WHO WORK WITH HIGH SCHOOLERS ARE READY TO HAND OFF ANOTHER SENIOR CLASS AND THEY ARE ROTATING BACK TO WORKING WITH FRESHMEN.

MAYBE SOMEONE FINALLY GOT A CO-LEADER FOR THEIR GROUP AND THEY THINK THAT IS TIME TO HAND THEM OFF TO THAT CO-LEADER.

The truth about all of the above is, it's an emotional process.

EVEN IF YOU MOVE ON QUICKLY WHEN YOU REPLACE YOURSELF, UNDERSTAND EVERY ONE OF YOUR VOLUNTEERS IS GOING TO HAVE A VARYING DEGREE OF EMOTION RELATED TO REPLACING THEMSELVES. AND THE LONGER THEIR TENURE IS, THE MORE EMOTION THAT WILL BE WRAPPED UP IN IT.

You should take that into consideration with each conversation you have, each opportunity you have to recognize, and each time you ponder the future.

As a leader you should:

Take the person replacing themselves to coffee or soft drinks and have a conversation about how they are dealing with this and talk about what is next in their life.

Recognize what they have done, and their time serving with the other volunteers in the department. Hopefully one day they will see that it will be okay to replace themselves too.

Be cautious about your excitement when new volunteers step up to take over. Even though we should celebrate this, we never want to do it at the expense of the volunteer who is being replaced.

Whether you think emotion related to this is good or bad, you need to understand that it is real. These people have given their time, for free, to a cause that they passionately believe in. It's emotional.

It's kind of like leaving the first house that you ever bought.

IT WAS A GREAT PLACE.

YOU MAY NEVER BE ABLE TO REPLACE THE MEMORIES.

YOU MIGHT HAVE BROUGHT YOUR FIRST CHILD HOME TO THIS HOUSE.

NAMES MIGHT HAVE BEEN CARVED INTO THE CEMENT ON THE SIDEWALK.

But now it's too small.

IT'S TOO FAR FROM WORK.

NOT ENOUGH BATHROOMS.

TOO MUCH LAWN TO MOW.

THE BASEMENT IS HAUNTED.

THE NEIGHBORS ARE WEIRD.

TIMES HAVE CHANGED.

AND IT'S TIME TO MOVE ON.

AND YOU MOVE ONTO SOMETHING BETTER. BUT THE PROCESS IN MOVING TO SOMETHING BETTER IS A HEAVY, EMOTIONAL DECISION. MAKE SURE TO SURROUND YOUR VOLUNTEERS WITH LOVE AS THEY GO THROUGH THAT PROCESS.

5. REPLACE YOURSELF

If you are encouraging your volunteers to replace themselves, then there is an important principle we need you to understand. There will come a time when you won't be in your current position either, just like them.

You might still be at the same church, or maybe you will move on to a different one. But this fact is true about all of us. There will come a time when someone else is doing the job you are doing now.

Here are three ways you might lay the groundwork for this.

1. HAVE CONVERSATIONS WITH LEADERS ABOVE YOU TO SHARE YOUR HEART WITH THEM.

Be open and honest when you think the time is right, explaining the idea of replacing yourself. If you are feeling a stirring in your life related to your position and you might be ready to move on to what is next, talk to your up-line leaders about it. Get their perspective on where you are as a leader and see if they have any thoughts about what is next for you. Have this conversation (maybe multiple conversations) before it's imminent so it's not a shock, but part of the culture. Then show how you can help transition well. (We know some leaders who quietly started replacing themselves five years in advance. Now that's planning!)

2. LOOK FOR MOVERS AND SHAKERS WHO ARE UP AND COMING.

Don't get so wrapped up in your day-to-day operational tasks that you forget to look around and see who is becoming a rock star in your ministry or department. There are volunteers that are excelling all around you and we should recognize their accomplishments, invest in them, and pray to see if perhaps something is stirring in their life which would lead them to take their leadership to the next level.

We love to hear stories about . . .

TEENAGERS WHO STARTED AS VOLUNTEERS AND NOW ARE LEADING PROGRAMS.

FOLKS WHO STARTED VOLUNTEERING BUT HAD A PROFESSIONAL CAREER AND THEN TRANSITIONED INTO A FULL-TIME POSITION AT CHURCH WHERE THEY STARTED VOLUNTEERS.

COLLEGE STUDENTS WHO PLANNED TO GO INTO A CAREER BUT CHANGED DIRECTIONS ALL BECAUSE SOMEONE NOTICED THEIR AWESOME ABILITY WHILE THEY WERE VOLUNTEERING.

Future church leaders might be incredible volunteers right now. Notice them.

3. GET AN APPRENTICE FOR YOURSELF.

This can be a very challenging process as you begin to let go of what you have to move on to what is next for you. But it is essential if you want to leave well. When you make the decision that it is time to move on to a new position or a new organization, it will be a great idea for you to get an apprentice to help set them up well. Don't start too soon, though. Make sure this apprenticing process doesn't go on forever though, no one wants to be there for too long.

TAKE A LOOK AT THE STEPS LISTED IN THE PREVIOUS PAGES AND HOW WE DETAILED OUT WHAT AN APPRENTICING PROCESS SHOULD LOOK LIKE. SEE IF THAT CAN TRANSLATE INTO SOMETHING FOR YOU AS YOU DECIDE TO REPLACE YOURSELF.

CHAPTER 7

YOU CAN'T ALWAYS SEE IT

THE SCOOP

When we see something that is unjust, or someone who needs help, we want to fix it or THEM right away. Instant results. Bada Bing, Bada Boom! The truth is that it doesn't happen that fast.

And when THAT doesn't happen, then THIS happens:

LINDA QUIT VOLUNTEERING WITH TODDLERS BECAUSE IT DIDN'T SEEM IMPORTANT.

TOM STOPPED SHOWING UP FOR MIDDLE SCHOOLERS BECAUSE NO ONE WAS CHANGING.

BOB TOLD HIS COACH THAT HE DIDN'T FEEL LIKE A VERY GOOD SPECIAL NEEDS LEADER.

CAROLE GAVE UP HER HIGH SCHOOL GIRLS GROUP BECAUSE THEY WANTED TO TALK MORE ABOUT BOYS THAN A RELATIONSHIP WITH GOD.

JEREMY EMAILED HIS RESIGNATION SAYING THAT HOLDING BABIES ON SUNDAY DIDN'T SEEM VERY SPIRITUAL.

That seems pretty normal to us, but then we have to ask a question.

What went wrong?

In each of these situations, volunteers signed up to help build faith in the next generation. Week after week they showed up but didn't see any tangible results. There wasn't anything they could point to that would validate the time

(WHAT WE TOLD YOUR VOLUNTEERS)

they were spending each week. So they assumed what they were doing wasn't significant and they quit.

The majority of time we don't get to hear the rest of each person's faith story.

But we have a Heavenly Father who sees all of that, and is planning a big reveal for us one day.

In Heaven we will find out the rest of each story, and see how important the part we played was. We'll understand that what we were doing in our volunteer role had long lasting impact in that person's life. You just have to believe that we are in for some incredible surprises when all of that becomes known.

Not only does our Heavenly Father see everything, He also knows everything we've done along the way as well. The big and the small. He is aware.

We have to be willing to go the distance in order to get the satisfaction that comes after all the time and effort.

RUN WITH IT

(HOW YOU HELP YOUR VOLUNTEERS DO IT)

1. FILL THE BUCKET (VISION LEAKS)

You have to continually remind volunteers of why they do what they do. You can never do this too often enough. Vision is where you are leading people. And people are wanderers. They wander so easily if they are not led in the right direction. We have to remind them of where we are going and how essential their role is in the process.

SMALL GROUP LEADERS NEED TO BE REMINDED HOW IMPORTANT THEIR FEW ARE, AND HOW THEY MIGHT BE THE SOLE SPIRITUAL INFLUENCE IN SOME OF THOSE LIVES.

Bible storytellers need to be reminded time and time again that one of the worst things that we can do is make Scripture boring and irrelevant for children. Their role is to make the text come alive so kids can have a real shot at understanding that this text is not dead and is more alive and relevant than ever.

Parking lot attendants need to be reminded they're the first impression every week, even if they might occasionally receive an awkward hand signal from drivers between the orange cones. And someone else might come back to church because they saw their smiling face on the way in.

That's why it's important to:

REPEAT THE VISION AGAIN AND AGAIN.

TAKE YOUR VOLUNTEERS TO CONFERENCES.

COMMUNICATE WHAT A WIN LOOKS LIKE.

GIVE THEM THE TOOLS THEY NEED.

ENCOURAGE THEM TO ATTEND KID OR STUDENT CAMP WITH OTHER LEADERS.

SPEND MEANINGFUL TIME WITH THEM.

FEED THEM DOUGHNUTS.

CONNECT THEM WITH OTHER KEY VOLUNTEERS.

It is so important for you to remind them, week in and week out, month in and month out, year in and year out, about how essential it is that they do what they do.

Because the truth is, they forget.

They get discouraged.

They get tired.

They get worn out.

They run out of doughnuts.

IT IS OUR JOB TO LOOK AT VISION LIKE A BUCKET WITH A HOLE IN IT.

(You've probably heard this analogy before.) A bucket with a hole in it, filled with water, will always run out unless you keep filling it back up. It will eventually become empty, incapable of serving its purpose.

We don't want anyone thinking that their purpose is pointless, because we know that what they are doing is actually priceless.

Don't let all the vision leak out, even if you get tired. Make it one of your primary roles or you might end up with volunteers who are like empty buckets.

2. RECOGNIZE TENURE

Your volunteers are never going to admit they volunteer to get something out of it for themselves. And most of them serve with a selfless attitude toward volunteering. But it doesn't hurt, and makes some of us feel pretty good, when someone recognizes what we have done. Other people like it, too.

NOT ONLY DOES THE VOLUNTEER FEEL APPRECIATED, BUT IT CREATES AN OPPORTUNITY FOR OTHER VOLUNTEERS TO RALLY AROUND AND IMAGINE A FUTURE OF THEIR OWN.

We know of a couple leading a small group who take the birthday thing to a whole new level. Not only do they send birthday cards to everyone in their second grade small group each year, they do it every year after that as well. Forever. One of these former second graders, who is now 31, recently posted on Facebook: "Ray and Mary first sent me a birthday card when I was in their second grade Sunday School class. And they haven't missed a year since . . . 23 cards thus far! Thank you!"

Or another volunteer named Dona-vive who recently passed away after serving in the infant nursery for over forty years. She slowed down as she got older, but was she ever committed to the infants in that room. Every single time the church did Baby Dedication, Dona-vive would sit on the front row and the leader of the department would say thank you to her. After years of doing this, some began to ask, "Why do they keep saying thank you to her?" But every bit of it was sincere.

Dona-vive was the longest serving volunteer in the history of the church. She had changed thousands of diapers and rocked thousands of babies. She deserved every moment in the spotlight given to her, and her legend grew greater as people remembered her and every life she touched.

It is important for you to recognize a volunteer who has given years and years of their life to the cause that they serve.

This not only pays homage to the legacy they have left, but it allows other volunteers who might be new to the game to see that they can stay in it for the long haul as well.

One of the best recognition events we have seen is an Academy Awards-style show where you have categories to recognize volunteers. Subsequently, at each of the award shows, a lifetime achievement award is given to someone who has served for an extended length. Generally, there isn't a dry eye in the room.

RECOGNIZING TENURE CAN PUT SOME CHANGE IN YOUR POCKET WITH VOLUNTEERS WHO HAVE BEEN AROUND FOR A WHILE AND CAN HELP NEW VOLUNTEERS SHOOT FOR THE MOON AND STAY IN IT.

3. CELEBRATE THE THINGS YOU CAN SEE

We told your volunteers that they may never see the results of their efforts here on Earth, and we meant it. They will go throughout their volunteer careers and hear very few people say:

"THANK YOU FOR OPENING MY EYES TO THE GOSPEL. IT TRANSFORMED ME."

- FROM PRESCHOOLERS.

"YOU ARE SO COOL. WOULD YOU LIKE TO COME TO PRESENT A PORTION OF WHAT WE DO IN SMALL GROUP AT MY CLASS?"

- FROM A FIFTH GRADE BOY.

"HELPING ME TO MAKE WISE CHOICES REALLY SET ME UP FOR THE BEST FUTURE I COULD POSSIBLY HAVE. THANK YOU FROM THE BOTTOM OF MY HEART."

– FROM A HIGH SCHOOL SENIOR.

Volunteers will not get a lot of direct admiration from those that they serve. They may never get to see the end of a person's faith story. They will never know what happens down the road when someone finally "gets it" and makes a decision that sets them on the right path.

EVEN THOUGH WE MAY NEVER SEE THOSE MOMENTS,

THERE ARE MOMENTS THAT WE CAN SEE.

We see all kinds of moments happen in families.

BABY DEDICATIONS.

BAPTISMS.

RECONCILIATIONS.

SALVATIONS.

PARENTING VICTORIES.

GRADUATIONS.

BIRTHDAY PARTIES.

WEDDINGS.

MILESTONE TRANSITIONS.

And a whole lot more.

The real question is this: Are you leading your volunteers to understand how crucial of a role they have had in these events?

This is why it is so important to . . .

INVOLVE SMALL GROUP LEADERS IN THE PROCESS OF A CHILD BEING BAPTIZED.

INVITE PRESCHOOL WORKERS TO BABY DEDICATION, SO THEY SEE PARENTS EXCITED ABOUT THE WORK THEY DO.

TELL THE STORIES OF FAMILIES WHO ARE HEALED, TRANSFORMED BY GOD, BECAUSE OF THE WORK OF YOUR MINISTRY.

When volunteers see that these things are actually happening, it reverses the trend from "You can't always see it" to "Wow, we actually can see some things happening!"

Some of these things are very public events like a baby dedication and baptism, but some are not public events. If a family is reconciled or there was an issue that people might not know about publicly, it might not be appropriate to share. These are the moments where you take a volunteer to coffee or lunch and talk about how essential he or she was in that process of restoration and redemption.

Think about this for a moment. You are a volunteer and you know families that you serve are having issues. Then your leader comes and asks you to have lunch. While at lunch, he or she tells you that you had a direct role in helping a family reconcile and now they are on a path to a better future. Would that excite you?

Here is the catch.

Leaders have to look for opportunities to do this. You won't always see every story, but they are there. Stories do exist.

ALL YOU NEED TO DO IS SHARE THEM, IN THE APPROPRIATE FORUM, FOR PEOPLE TO REALIZE THEY CAN SOMETIMES SEE IT.

4. KEEP STORIES ROLLING IN

Just because you have told a few stories doesn't mean you have completed your job. You have to constantly seek out stories to put in front of your people. And trust us, this can be exhausting and leave you wondering, "Can I just make one up today?" No, you can't (and every single story in this book is true!)

KEEP TELLING THE STORIES THAT ROLL IN.

We are going to be honest with you: Finding stories over and over again can wipe you out, because these stories don't just need to be found, they need to be told.

TELLING STORIES TAKES TIME.

TELLING STORIES TAKES ENERGY.

TELLING STORIES TAKES EFFORT.

TELLING STORIES TAKES IT OUT OF YOU.

But, it's worth it. Every single time.

We believe that stories, when told over time, offer someone a sense of perspective. When your volunteers have perspective, they see the big impact of the little things and the little details of the big things.

This is why it is so important for you to keep these stories rolling in. Put this in your reminders app and have it notify you every week that you need to keep finding and telling stories of what it looks like to win.

That notification will annoy you after awhile, but it is one of the most important notifications you will read each week. (Plus you'll have a story to tell about how annoying your reminders app is).

5. SAY NO (HELP TO PROTECT YOUR VOLUNTEERS)

If you are going to keep volunteers in the game for a long time, then you have to protect them and keep them focused. We tend to look at a career of volunteering as more of a marathon than a sprint. If you have ever run a marathon you know what we are talking about.

Marathons take a lot of time to complete. Whether you are running a half at 13.1 miles or a full marathon at 26.2 miles, it is difficult to finish either one. We asked some of the best runners we know what were some of the mistakes that they've made during marathons. Here is what they told us.

THEY STARTED OUT TOO STRONG AND WERE WINDED BY MILE NUMBER THREE.

THEY TRIED TO PICK UP STEAM IN THE MIDDLE OF THE RACE ONLY TO CRASH AND BURN ALONG THE WAY.

THE MOST IMPORTANT THING THEY DID WAS STOP FOR THE CUP OF WATER.

We compared what they told us to volunteering for the long haul.

THEY STARTED OUT TOO STRONG AND WERE WINDED BY MILE NUMBER THREE.

Many people start out slowly with volunteering. They just want to dip their big toe in the water and see if it is for them. But every so often you get that person who jumps in with both feet, maybe a little too fast. They take on multiple volunteering positions with multiple departments. This will lead to burnout on behalf of the volunteer and bickering amongst staff members who lead those departments over the volunteer's time.

Help your volunteers focus and not to over-commit. They need to get passionate about one thing and stick with it. That will help them stay in it for the long haul, even when they can't always see it.

THEY TRIED TO PICK UP STEAM IN THE MIDDLE OF THE RACE ONLY TO CRASH AND BURN ALONG THE WAY.

Volunteers who have been in the game for a while often desire a change or sense a need to pick up the pace. Maybe they need to try something different. Some people even say, "I am going to keep doing what I am doing and then add something new on to see if I like it."

But this can lead them off track.

If they want to pick up the pace of their volunteering in the middle of the race, we suggest you lead them to take on a more detailed leadership position where they are already volunteering. Instead of being a small group leader in K-5 and wanting to add on another group of high school girls, suggest they become a coach of elementary small group leaders. Instead of wanting to be a parking lot attendant and an usher, maybe you encourage the volunteer to lead a team of parking lot volunteers.

THE MOST IMPORTANT THING THEY DID WAS STOP FOR THE CUP OF WATER.

The title of this section is to say no, but we actually think sometimes you should say yes to taking a break. We hit on this a little bit in Chapter 6 under "Seasonal Volunteering," but there are times in a person's life when they need to stop, take a drink of water, and then start again. It is only natural for the human body to run out of energy and excitement. What if the best thing you could do for volunteers was to give them a break? Whether it is a month, three months, or an entire year. Maybe a break is something that they need to come back refreshed and ready to go.

Maybe . . .

YOU GIVE ALL WEEKLY VOLUNTEERS THE SUMMER OFF— EVERY YEAR.

YOU GIVE VOLUNTEERS WHO HAVE BEEN SERVING FIVE YEARS OR MORE A FRIENDLY ASSESSMENT TO SEE HOW THEY CAN ADVANCE THEIR LEADERSHIP.

YOU GIVE VOLUNTEERS WHO HAVE BEEN IN THE GAME TEN YEARS A FULL YEAR OFF TO RECHARGE THEIR BATTERIES. (WITH A CONDITION TO RETURN, OF COURSE.)

Volunteering is a marathon, not a sprint. Help your volunteers run like it. It is your job to protect your volunteers by helping them say no when they begin, and throughout their time. When they focus on one thing, advance their leadership, and take a break when they need it, they will be the volunteers who stay in the game long enough to see it.

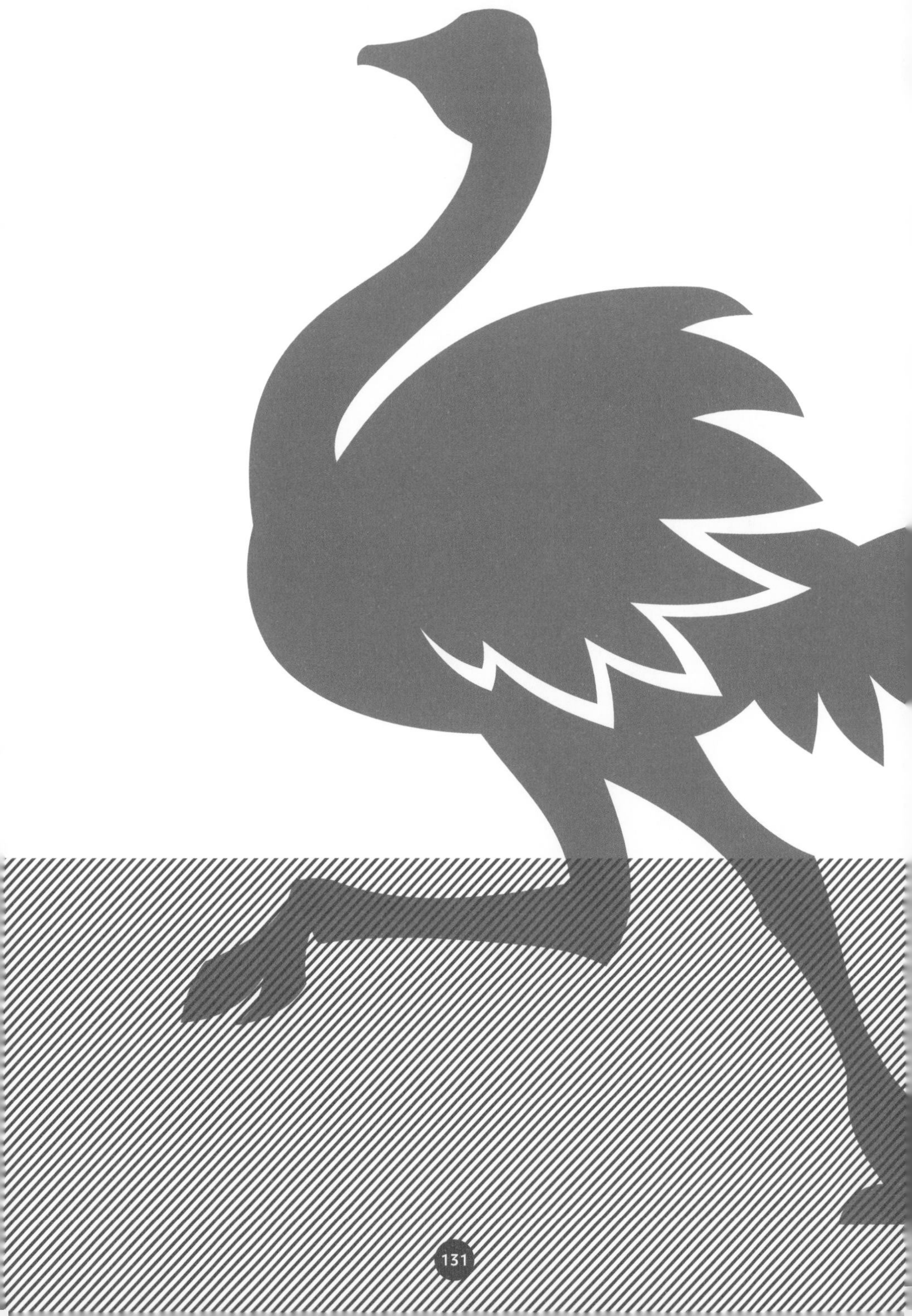

ONE LAST
NOT NORMAL WORD

Leaders, when is the last time a volunteer served you? Think of a time a volunteer showed up just in the nick of time to . . .

BRING A MEAL,

WATCH YOUR KIDS,

HELP YOUR OWN HIGH SCHOOL STUDENT THROUGH A FAITH CRISIS,

ENCOURAGE YOU AS A PARENT,

SIT WITH YOU AT THE HOSPITAL,

MEET YOU FOR COFFEE AFTER A ROUGH DAY,

MAKE YOU LAUGH ABOUT IT,

TELL YOU WHAT YOU ARE DOING RIGHT,

OR PRAY FOR YOU?

DO YOU REMEMBER HOW YOU FELT AFTERWARD?

INCREDIBLE APPRECIATION

DEEP DOWN GRATEFULNESS

HUGE RELIEF

BEST MEAL EVER!

ENCOURAGED TO LEAD ANOTHER DAY

VALUED

LIKE THEY SAVED THE DAY

Exactly.

That's how your not normal volunteers make others feel when they serve. They are faith-builders. They are homes for the homeless. They are Christmas boxes for those who live with the bare minimum. They are hope-givers to those ready to give up. They are friends to kids with special challenges. And God has given YOU the incredible privilege of leading these volunteers to be all that they can be in this world.

It's time for you to understand how important what you do is. It is the most important leadership thing that you will ever do. These volunteers are the people serving the families inside and outside the walls of your church.

Ready to get down to work?

LEAD STRONG, NOT NORMAL LEADER. LEAD STRONG.

Until our job here is done.

ABOUT THE AUTHORS

SUE MILLER

Sue is a teacher, leader, speaker, and author with a passion for bringing out the best in volunteers. Much of that passion developed over the 17 years she served as Children's Ministry Director at Willow Creek Community Church near Chicago, Illinois. Her ongoing challenge was to figure out how to recruit, grow, and keep a fantastic team of volunteers that could influence the faith of the 3,000 kids that attended each weekend. She also served on the senior management team under the leadership of pastor Bill Hybels, a champion of volunteerism.

In 2005, Sue joined Orange, a nonprofit organization that creates resources to help churches partner with parents to build faith in the next generation. She's traveled all over the world helping parents and churches develop life-changing experiences for children and teenagers.

Currently she and Adam work with a team to create Live to Serve conferences. These are one-day training events for volunteers that are creative, informative, and impactful (fun too!) Sue is the author of several books, including *Parenting Is Wonder-full*, *Making Your Children's Ministry the Best Hour of Every Kid's Week,* and *Not Normal: 7 Quirks of Incredible Volunteers.*

When not working, Sue lives with her handsome husband, Rick, in a fixer-upper house in Atlanta, Georgia. She does life with her two favorite adult kids, one amazing son-in-law, a mischievous black mini schnauzer and two of the most incredible grandsons on the planet.

ADAM DUCKWORTH

Adam is the Lead Communicator at Downtown Harbor Church in Fort Lauderdale, a church that is aiming to REDEFINE the church experience in the city of Fort Lauderdale. Adam transitioned to that role in April of 2015 after spending 15 years leading innovative Children & Family Ministry departments in Michigan and Florida.

Before launching a career of leading volunteers at a church, Adam attended the University of Toledo, where he completed degrees in both education and English.

Adam recently co-authored *Not Normal: 7 Quirks of Incredible Volunteers* with Sue Miller and he loves traveling to churches with Live to Serve to inspire and help volunteers up their game. Additionally, Adam hosts the Studio 252 program and serves as a communicator at Camp KidJam, Orange Conference, and Orange Tour. He is also the Owner/Operator of Travelmation LLC, a Disney-specific Travel Agency which aims to "Help Families Make Magical Memories."

Adam lives a block from the beach in Fort Lauderdale with his wife, Katelyn, and their petite goldendoodle, Dottie. For more information about Adam, follow him on Twitter @adam_duckworth.

TEACH YOUR TEAM THE SEVEN QUIRKS OF INCREDIBLE VOLUNTEERS.

BECAUSE YOUR VOLUNTEERS ARE
NOT NORMAL.

Quantity discounts available at:
www.OrangeStore.org

(a perfect gift for your quirky volunteers)

GO weekly

DEVELOP SMALL GROUP LEADERS & ENGAGE PARENTS
in TWO hours a week.

 videos

 interviews

 e-books

 podcasts

 emails

 social media plans

SIGN UP TODAY AT GoWeekly.com!

Oh, and we almost forgot.

When you subscribe to Weekly, you'll get another tool to help you SEND your small group leaders what they need to know every week—the ability to customize the Lead Small App.